Making Wom

The Interrogation of Palestinian Women Security Detainees
by
the Israeli General Security Services

To the many women who told me their stories

Making Women Talk

The Interrogation of Palestinian Women Security Detainees by The Israeli General Security Services

*

Teresa Thornhill

with a foreword by Geoffrey Bindman

Lawyers For Palestinian Human Rights

Box BMJPI, • London WC1N 3XX

Published in England by Lawyers for Palestinian Human Rights,
Box BMJPI, London WC1N 3XX

Cover designed by Lee Robinson

Typeset by Idiom

Printed by Biddles Limited, Walnut Tree House,
Woodbridge Park, Guildford, Surrey GU1 1DA

Distributed in UK by Turnaround,
27 Horsell Road, London N5 1XL

British Library Cataloguing in Publication Data

Thornhill, Teresa
Making Women Talk: Interrogation of
Palestinian Women Detainees by the
Israeli General Security Services

I. Title
323.40956

ISBN 0-9519610-0-4

Contents

Acknowledgements*

The help of the following people is gratefully acknowledged:-

Stan Cohen, Daniel Machover, Penny Maddrell, Ayad Rahim, Anne Rodford, Liz Veats; members of staff at al-Haq and at the Association for Civil Rights in Israel; Palestinian and Israeli lawyers Jawad Boulos, Felicia Langer, Mohammed Na'amne, Mona Rishmawi, Leah Tsemel, Salma Wakim.

The help of the following organizations is gratefully acknowledged:- the Palestine Human Rights Information Centre for the use of facilities at their East Jerusalem office; and the Chambers of Ian McDonald QC and Owen Davies, for financial assistance.

Israel and the Occupied Territories
LEBANON
SYRIAN ARAB REPUBLIC
GOLAN
Jalama
Haifa
Tiberias
Nazareth
Mediterranean Sea
Jordan
Jenin
Netanya
Tulkarm
Nablus
Tel Mond
Qalqilya
WEST BANK
Tel Aviv
Petakh Tikva
Amman
Ramallah
Ramla
Jericho
Jerusalem
Bethlehem
Ashkelon
Dead Sea
Hebron
Gaza
GAZA
Rafah
Beersheba
JORDAN
ISRAEL
EGYPT
N
W
E
S
0 10 20 30 40 km
0 10 20 30 40 miles
Elat

I could hear sounds from where I was inside the 'Coffin'. There was a slow knocking sound which seemed to come from deep inside the wall. There was a sound of a snake hissing and the sound of deep crying. I heard sounds like that, for a long time.

This experience of the 'Coffin' is intended to destroy the prisoner from inside. You feel that you are very far from all of your family and from all of your friends, in a place where you are at the mercy of two or three Shabak *officers who have ugly faces and an ugly way of treating people.*

Maha Nassar

"Representatives of the Women's Committee in Beit Jala visit martyrs graves to lay wreaths, on the second anniversary of the outbreak of the *intifada.*"

Photographer: *Nadia Sultani*

Foreword

At the end of the First World War, Palestine was inhabited by about six hundred thousand Arabs and about sixty seven thousand Jews. Large-scale Jewish immigration began at the end of the nineteenth century, with the emergence of the Zionist movement in response to a new wave of anti-Jewish activity in Europe. In 1922, following the ending of Ottoman rule, Palestine was placed under the British Mandate. By 1945, Mandate Palestine had a population of about two million, of whom two thirds were Arabs and one third were Jews.

In 1947, the UN General Assembly passed a resolution recommending termination of the Mandate under a partition plan. The plan was not accepted by the Arabs but the Mandate expired on 14 May 1948 and the State of Israel was proclaimed on the following day.

War followed, at the end of which the boundaries of the State of Israel were set according to the Armistice lines of 1949.

The Gaza Strip and the West Bank, which had formed part of the Mandate, fell outside the new state. For the next eighteen years, the Gaza Strip was administered by Egypt and the West Bank by Jordan, although the sovereignty of both territories remained unresolved. Most Arabs living within the boundaries of Israel who had not fled during the war, became Israeli citizens.

During the Six Days' War in June 1967, Israel occupied the Gaza Strip, the West Bank and East Jerusalem ("the Occupied Territories"). It also occupied the Golan Heights and the Sinai peninsula, which had been part of the sovereign territories of Syria and Egypt respectively. In 1978, Israel withdrew from the Sinai peninsula, under the Camp David peace accords. It remains in occupation of the Golan Heights and the Occupied Territories.

The Declaration on the Establishment of the State of Israel of 14 May 1948 promised that the new country would be developed for the benefit of all its inhabitants, and that it would maintain complete equality of political and social rights of all its citizens, irrespective of race, religion or sex.

There is no reason to doubt that for many Jewish Israelis those aspirations were sincere, and there are many today who would wish their government to uphold them. Sadly it is all too evident even within the pre-1967 boundaries of Israel that Arab citizens suffer severely unequal treatment in many respects.

The treatment during interrogation of Palestinian women detainees from the Occupied Territories is comprehensively documented for the first time in this book. The excesses and abuses described demonstrate a disregard for basic human rights which mocks the ideals of the founders of the State and disgraces the Israeli government which must take responsibility for them.

Torture, however, is only one of a range of measures used to suppress and intimidate those who oppose the occupation and seek some form of Palestinian independence. Other measures include wilful killing, arbitrary arrest, punitive demolition of homes, deportations and the forced separation of families.

By denying that it is bound by the Fourth Geneva Convention of 1949 – the internationally agreed standard for the treatment of civilians in time of war – the Israeli government claims to be entitled to adopt these measures. Its own Supreme Court (in a distressing departure from an otherwise respectable reputation for independence) is virtually alone in the world among legal authorities in regarding Israel as exempt from liability under the Convention.

Torture is not merely an instrument of repression. It is a crucial link in a process of criminalization of the Palestinian population which resembles the strategies pursued by security forces against the black population of South Africa, and, doubtless to a lesser extent, against members of the Catholic community in Northern Ireland. In Britain, false confessions secured by police pressure were responsible for several of the rash of miscarriages of justice recently recognized by the Court of Appeal – the Birmingham Six, the Guildford Four, and the Broadwater Farm Three. The confession extracted by torture out of public view is a tried and tested method of fulfilling the requirements of legal proof. But, in Israel as elsewhere, it is a spurious legality. Far from upholding the rule of law, such abuses pervert and destroy it.

There is an imperative need for the barbarous practices revealed in this book to be swiftly ended. As is explained in Chapter Four, a report bearing the name of a former President of the Israeli Supreme Court may have encouraged the belief in the occupying forces that torture is lawful. The Supreme Court has also found it difficult to establish effective jurisdiction over the military authorities in the Occupied Territories. Thus it may be unrealistic to expect the Israeli military courts to intervene. So, at the end of the day, the responsibility lies with the government of Israel to act, and with the international community to use all possible pressure to make it do so.

Geoffrey Bindman
London
July 1992

A Note on the Research Methods

The nineteen statements on which this report is based were collected during the spring and summer of 1990, from a wide range of women and girls aged 14 to 41. All were in detention on dates between 1986 and 1990. They fall into three groups. Fourteen were Palestinians from East Jerusalem, the West Bank and Gaza. Three were Palestinian Israelis. Finally, two were Jewish Israeli women peace activists who were interrogated for security offences. Where possible, the interrogation methods used on the three groups are compared.

At the outset of the research project, contact was made with the four Palestinian women's committees. [1] Each committee was invited to provide introductions to women who had been interrogated by the General Security Services and who might be willing to tell their stories. In addition, some contacts were provided by individuals. All contacts offered were followed up, although attempts to meet with women in the West Bank and Gaza were sometimes hampered by strikes and curfews and therefore not every contact resulted in an interview taking place. Contacts with the Palestinian Israeli and Jewish Israeli women were provided by individuals.

Most of the statements were taken by the author, on the basis of one or two interviews with the woman concerned. Some of the statements are in the form of affidavits[2] taken by the woman's lawyer whilst she was in detention. One statement (which appears in Appendix III) was taken by al-Haq[3], and is quoted with their permission.

The affidavits were taken in Arabic but were given to the author having been translated into English. The statement taken by al-Haq in Arabic was translated into English by the Palestine Human Rights Information Centre translation unit. Of the interviews conducted by the author, some were conducted in English (when the interviewee had a good command of English). Others were conducted with the assistance of a Palestinian in the locality who spoke good English. The quality of translation varied, inevitably. The points in any interview which seemed to be of most significance were gone over as thoroughly as possible. It is probable that inaccuracies occurred in translation of certain terms. For example, if an interviewee was arrested by a member of the police force, she may nevertheless have described that person as a "soldier", or the term "policeman" may have been translated as "soldier". This reflects a pervasive attitude on the part of many Palestinians who, understandably, do not distinguish between different types of Israeli security personnel.

Such details were not considered to be of major importance, for the purposes of this report.

All statements are quoted with the permission of the woman concerned or, in a few cases where the woman was unavailable, her lawyer. In a very few cases, anonymity was requested and a pseudonym has been used; in all other cases, the women's real names are used. Appendix IV gives background information about each woman.

It is perhaps necessary to stress that, although the interviews were carried out two years ago and some of the affidavits refer to interrogations which occurred even longer ago, there is ample evidence that the same methods of interrogation are still in regular use. The monthly bulletins issued by the Israeli group "Women's Organization for Women Political Prisoners", among other sources, confirm this.

July 1992

Notes

1. The committees are:- The Union of Palestinian Women's Committees; The Association of Women's Committees for Social Work; The Union of Palestinian Women's Action Committees; The Union of Working Women's Committees.
2. When a statement is referred to as an 'affidavit' it means that, having given the statement, the woman swore in the presence of a lawyer that the contents of the statement were true.
3. Al-Haq is a Palestinian human rights organisation, and is the West Bank affiliate of the International Commission of Jurists.

Introduction

One of the tools with which Israel attempts to suppress nationalist activity by Palestinians, both those from the Occupied Territories and those who are Israeli citizens, is the detention, interrogation[1] and prosecution of individuals on so-called 'security' charges.[2]

A separate legal system operates in the West Bank and Gaza from that inside Israel. In both systems, 'security' legislation is sufficiently wide-ranging to criminalize a number of activities which are political in nature and which cannot be said to endanger either state security or that of the occupation forces. In addition, it criminalizes acts of violence against both of these.

It appears that one of the purposes of 'security' trials is to keep a high percentage of politically-minded Palestinians in prison, for long periods of time, with a limited regard to whether or not they are actually guilty of the offences charged. Palestinians from the West Bank and Gaza Strip charged with 'security' offences are tried in military courts set up by the Israelis since 1967. The Israeli military justice system falls very far short of internationally accepted norms for the protection of the defendant's right to a fair trial. The system has been described by lawyers who have practised in it as a "sham" and a "charade".

The vast majority of Palestinians arrested in connection with security offences are male, (and are residents of the Occupied Territories, as opposed to Arab citizens of Israel). From a total of 79,000 Palestinians thought to have been arrested between the start of the *intifada* on 9 December 1987 and 1 September 1991, only some three thousand were women.[3]

However, considerably more women have been arrested during the *intifada* than during the years immediately before it began. This is a reflection of the increasing involvement of women in political activity.[4]

This report addresses the widespread allegations of sexual harassment, beatings and torture during interrogation of Palestinian women 'security' detainees.[5] Such allegations have been made both by women from the Occupied West Bank and Gaza and by Palestinian Israelis. If these allegations are true, not only are the women suffering physically and mentally during the interrogation period, but also, for those who are charged and tried, the chances of a fair trial must be very seriously prejudiced. For, if a woman makes a confession as a result of abuse during interrogation, it is almost impossible to retract it afterwards, and a conviction on the basis of it is a near-certainty. The law allows a defendant to challenge the admissibility of a confession, in a *voir dire* or 'mini-trial'. However, the nature of security trials is such that it is almost unheard of for a defendant to win a *voir dire*.

Sometimes a woman is strong enough not to make a confession statement despite abuse during interrogation, and there is rarely any independent evidence on the basis of which to charge her. In such a case, she may be released without charge. However, a common tactic used by the interrogators in this situation, is to obtain a statement incriminating the defendant from another detainee. It is widely alleged by ex-detainees and defence lawyers that these are also obtained under duress. A special rule of evidence in Israeli law allows convictions to stand on the basis of such statements.

The report is concerned with the particular methods used to obtain confessions and statements from Palestinian women and girls; the legality or otherwise of these methods; and the implications of their use for the defendant's exercise of her right to a fair trial, as recognized by international law.

In Chapter One the legal framework in which security offences are investigated and tried, is outlined. The military court system in the West Bank and Gaza is described, as are the parallel military and criminal jurisdictions inside Israel. The types of evidence used in the prosecution of security offences are considered, and the paramount importance of the obtaining of confessions is explained. The chapter ends by outlining the legal rules which ensure the complete isolation of the detainee during interrogation (for example, the restriction of lawyers' access to interrogees).

In Chapter Two the interrogation methods are described, with extensive quotes from the women's statements. The process of getting the woman into a state of mind in which she is likely to make a confession begins from the moment of arrest. In the interrogators' hands she is deprived of food, sleep and basic hygiene; subjected to various forms of physical abuse; threatened with rape and otherwise sexually harassed; and, if the woman is a mother, she is pressurized by the making of often false allegations about her children.

Chapter Three examines the impact of the interrogation methods on the defendant's right to a fair trial. We look at what happens when a woman tries to claim, at trial, that her confession was extracted under duress. Having found that a confession is almost invariably followed by a conviction, we consider what avenues of redress may be open to the woman who has been abused during interrogation. The limited effectiveness of making official complaints and the possibility of bringing civil actions in the courts are discussed. Lastly, in Chapter Four, the question 'does Israel sanction the use of torture?' is posed. The various international conventions which prohibit the practice of torture are considered. The Landau Commission Report, which recommended the use of psychological and "moderate physical" pressure during interrogation, is discussed in detail. The possibility of bringing complaints, prosecutions and civil actions against alleged perpetrators of abuse during interrogation, is examined. Lastly, the role of the international community in preventing the practice of torture is discussed.

Appendix I is a discussion of the legal concept of the 'right to a fair trial'. Appendix II outlines the relevant provisions of international humanitarian law. Appendix III gives background information about each of the women interviewed, together with details of their detentions. Appendix IV looks at special cases of female security prisoners who were pregnant when arrested and who appear to have miscarried as a result of their treatment during arrest and or while in custody. These cases came to light during the research done for the report, but are not all cases of maltreatment during interrogation. They are included here because they reflect a danger uniquely faced by female prisoners, and one which has not been well documented elsewhere.

Chapter One: The Legal Framework

Jurisdiction

Residents of the West Bank and Gaza charged with security offences are tried under military law in special military courts which were set up by the Israelis following the occupation in June 1967.[6]

Under Israeli military law, a wide range of offences are classed as "security" offences. They include: (a) offences specifically classified as such in Military Orders (some of which are clearly political, for example "the congregation of ten or more people for the purpose of discussing a political subject"[7], and "insulting behaviour towards an IDF officer"[8]); (b) criminal offences which may be security offences in some circumstances (for example failing to prevent an offence, distributing pamphlets, providing false information); and (c) offences against the military justice system (for example escaping from legal custody, contempt of court) and some financial offences (for example, failure to pay income tax, customs fraud).[9] Criminal offences which are not seen as having security implications are tried in the local Palestinian courts, which pre-date the occupation.

Palestinian residents of East Jerusalem[10] and all Israeli citizens are tried under Israeli law.

Within Israeli law there are two separate jurisdictions or legal systems under which defendants may be tried for offences with security implications. One jurisdiction is military, having its origins in the military judicial system which existed under the British. If a defendant is charged under military law[11] she or he will be tried in the one remaining military court which sits at Lod. If, on the other hand, she is charged under the regular criminal law then she will be tried in the criminal court (known as the 'District' court). Many of the same security offences appear in both military law and the criminal code.

The decision as to whether to try an individual Palestinian resident of East Jerusalem under the military or the criminal law is taken by the Attorney General. The most serious offences are tried under military law, but offences of stone throwing, for example, and even fire-bombing are usually tried under criminal law. The majority of Palestinians resident in East Jerusalem are therefore tried in the East Jerusalem District court, and relatively few at Lod. Proceedings begun in the District court can, however, be transferred to the military court.

Palestinian Israelis charged with security offences are sometimes tried in the military court. Although, in theory, Jewish Israelis can be tried in the military court, none has been since shortly after the beginning of the state. Jewish Israelis facing security charges are tried in the criminal courts.

The rules of evidence applied in the military courts, both those in the West Bank and Gaza and at Lod, are in most respects the same as those applied in the criminal courts. The military courts have greater powers of sentence than the criminal courts.

Where the law is set out in this report, a distinction is made between the provisions which apply in the West Bank and Gaza and those which apply inside Israel. Any reference to "Israeli law" may be taken as applying to Palestinian residents of East Jerusalem as well as to all Israeli citizens.

The Military Courts

Much has been written about the questionable nature of the justice dispensed by the Israeli military courts in the West Bank and Gaza. While the scope of this report does not allow for a thorough analysis of the system, the following points must be made. Firstly, both military court judges and prosecutors are Israeli Defence Force soldiers. This calls into question the impartiality of the judges. Secondly, the language of the court is Hebrew, which most defendants do not understand. Thirdly, defendants who contest the charges against them usually spend many months on remand before being brought to trial, which puts pressure on them to plead guilty (since a guilty plea will usually result in a shorter sentence and time served on remand is discounted from the sentence). In numerous ways, the military court process is weighted heavily in favour of the prosecution, so that the defendant has little or no chance of getting a fair trial.

The military court is presided over by either one or three judges. It is run by the army; the clerk and the interpreter are soldiers. Order is kept in court by soldiers, and the cells attached to the court are run by soldiers. An interpreter is usually present in court but translation of the proceedings is generally incomplete and poor in quality.[12]

The main difference between the military courts in the West Bank and Gaza on the one hand, and the one at Lod on the other hand, is that the former have a much heavier case load than the latter. Due to the vast numbers of Palestinians arrested and brought before the courts during the *intifada*, the military courts in the West Bank and Gaza have come to operate like assembly lines, processing huge numbers of defendants each day, with an almost total disregard for their legal and human rights. At Lod the pressures are less, and the quality of justice dispensed is perhaps somewhat better.

Evidence in Security Trials: The reliance on confessions

In regular criminal courts in most common law legal systems, criminal offences are prosecuted by the presentation to the court of the best evidence available. What evidence is available will depend on the investigation that has been carried out following the commission of the offence, usually by the police force. In the case of a murder, for example, the evidence may consist of eye-witness statements, forensic material collected at the relevant location, and any statement or confession made by the defendant to the police. In every case, the police should attempt to gather evidence of these three types, and it is relatively rare to found a prosecution solely on the evidence of an alleged confession by the defendant.

In the Israeli military judicial system, however, investigations are almost always limited to the interrogation of detainees with the aim of securing a confession to the offence in question (or sometimes, where this has been unsuccessful, the interrogation of another detainee with the aim of obtaining a statement incriminating the first detainee). Forensic evidence is rarely, if ever, sought, although in many cases it is difficult to see why it could not be obtained. In murder cases, for example, autopsies are very rarely performed, whereas in civilian legal systems they are standard practice. Likewise, eye-witness statements are rarely sought. The justification put forward by the authorities is that Palestinian witnesses are unwilling to come forward, which is true. However, in some cases there should be non-Palestinian eye-witnesses who could be called upon (for example Israeli soldiers and settlers).

The fact that the military prosecutors do not bother to obtain the fullest evidence available is consistent with the widely held view that the military justice system exists to serve a political function rather than one of genuine law-enforcement. According to this view, its function is to keep significant numbers of Palestinians behind bars, with all the repercussions in their communities which that entails. Whether those convicted are actually guilty of the offences in question, is not regarded by the authorities as being of paramount importance.

The obtaining of confessions, then, is clearly critical to the military judicial process.

The Interrogators

Most interrogation work is carried out by the General Security Services, Israel's internal intelligence agency (commonly known by the acronym *Shabak* or the Hebrew initials "Shin Bet".[13] According to the Israeli authorities, interrogation work is divided between the GSS and the regular police, according to the seriousness of the suspected offence. Minors are supposed to be interrogated by the police rather than the GSS. It appears that this is not the practice however, and that the majority of serious interrogation work is done by the GSS.[14] It is probably true to say that the GSS interrogate detainees suspected of involvement in organizations, whereas those detained for activities of a more spontaneous nature may be dealt with by the police. Homicide is always dealt with by the GSS.

Most women interviewed for this report believed that their interrogators were GSS members. For example, only one of the women interviewed for this report said that she was interviewed mainly by police officers, and she added that there was a GSS officer present. (Suha Sanduqa, who was interviewed at the age of 15 about an allegation of stone throwing).

The identity of the interrogators is important. Unlike the police, the GSS operate behind a veil of secrecy and are not publicly accountable. The police come under the control of the Ministry of Police. The names of their senior officers are publicly known and complaints regarding police conduct are made directly to them.[15] A similar system of accountability exists in the army. The army comes under the control of the Ministry of Defence and the identity of senior personnel is public information. There is a system for making complaints against army personnel and there is a public relations officer and a legal adviser who can be approached. Furthermore, the relevant Ministers can be questioned about police or army policy in the Knesset (the Israeli parliament).

It is not suggested that the complaints of individuals aggrieved by police or army conduct generally receive a satisfactory response, merely that there is a measure of public accountability.[16] The GSS, by comparison, appear to operate entirely outside the law. Indeed, legally speaking, the GSS barely exist. The law gives them virtually no powers or duties. Thus for example they have no power to arrest, detain or carry out searches. Almost everything which they need to do which could expose them to the public view, is done for them by the police.

The GSS do not come under the control of any Ministry. They report to the Prime Minister alone. The identity of all their personnel is kept strictly secret, including that of their director. A woman wishing to make a complaint about GSS conduct during interrogation faces the initial problem of not being able to identify the interrogators concerned, since they refer to themselves by pseudonyms (usually in Arabic). She then faces the problem that there is no direct public access to the GSS: she is obliged to make her complaint to one of three possible bodies, and it is not clear which of the three, if any, is under a legal duty to investigate her complaint. The three are: the commander of the detention centre where she was interrogated, who will be a police officer; the Prime Minister's office and the Attorney General.[17]

Probably the most important aspect of the lack of accountability of the GSS, is the fact that there is no law or publicly available code of practice to regulate their conduct of interrogations. The nearest approximation to a code of practice is the Appendix to the Landau Commission Report. This report, published in October 1987, condoned the use of "psychological and moderate physical pressure" by the GSS. An Appendix contains a set of guidelines for GSS methods in the light of these recommendations. However, it was intended that the Appendix should remain secret, and to date it has not been published. Moreover, the Landau Report and its Appendices do not have the force of law. Their legal status has, it seems, deliberately been left unclear (see Chapter Four).

The lack of public information on what the GSS are authorized to do to detainees during interrogation makes it very difficult to mount a legal challenge to their conduct.

Interrogation Centres

When a woman is arrested for interrogation, regardless of where she is from, she is taken to one of a number of detention centres inside Israel.[18] In general, women from Jerusalem and the central part of the West Bank are taken to the 'Russian Compound' ('Muskubiya') in Jerusalem; women from the north of the West Bank and Israel are mainly taken to Jalama Detention Centre, near Haifa; women from Gaza are usually taken to Ashkelon prison (south of Tel Aviv), and women are sometimes interrogated in the Abu Kabir Detention Centre in Tel Aviv. Sometimes a woman is moved several times during the interrogation period, for no apparent reason other than to disorientate her.

The overall control of each of these centres is not in the hands of the GSS, but of the police. The GSS has its own section within the larger centre. In theory the police have the right to enter the GSS section, but in practice they do not interfere at all. The GSS rule within their own section and the police turn a blind eye to anything they may learn of GSS methods and practices.[19]

Incommunicado Detention

During the interrogation period, which may last from a number of days to several months, the woman is held in total isolation in the GSS section. The public, of course, are strictly barred from entering. It is very difficult for lawyers to gain access to their clients in the GSS section, and family visits are not permitted. The detainee is not permitted to telephone or write to anybody. She is also carefully prevented from meeting other detainees (except, occasionally, 'collaborators'). The only contact she is likely to have with the outside world, is during her brief visit or visits to court to have her detention extended.

Consultations with Lawyers

It is very rare for a Palestinian detainee (whether male or female, from the Occupied Territories or inside Israel) to be allowed to see a lawyer during the interrogation period.[20]

The denial of access to a lawyer during interrogation can have very serious consequences for the fairness of the trial. For example, the first-time detainee may not be aware that she has a right to remain silent in the face of the interrogator's insistent questioning. This is a fundamental right. The interrogators are most unlikely to inform her of it. As has been said, there are no published rules concerning the conduct of interrogations, and thus it appears that Israeli law does not place the GSS under a legal duty to explain this right.

If the detainee is not given the opportunity to be advised by a lawyer of her right to silence, she may make a confession, and it will be practically impossible to retract it at a later stage.

The rules under which lawyers are prevented from visiting detainees under interrogation regarding security offences, are as follows. Residents of the West Bank and Gaza are *prima facie* entitled to see a lawyer as soon as possible after they request it. However, the "head of the investigation" (the interrogator in charge) is entitled, by a written order, to delay the visit for up to fifteen days from the date of arrest. A "confirming authority" is entitled to extend this period by a further fifteen days. Again a written order is required. In both cases, the criteria are "reasons of local security or the good of the investigation".

In addition to this, a judge may extend the period during which access to a lawyer is denied by up to thirty days (a cumulative total of sixty days). In addition, the President or Vice President of the court is entitled to extend this period by a further thirty days (to a sum total of ninety days) if the Commander of the Israeli Defence Force in the area has given written confirmation that special local security considerations demand this.[21]

For detainees held under Israeli law, the criteria and procedure for withholding lawyers' visits are the same, but the time periods are shorter. A GSS officer can, by a written order, delay the visit until seven days after the arrest; thereafter, a senior GSS officer can delay it for a further eight days, making a total of fifteen; a court may then order that the visit be delayed by a further fifteen days, making a total possible delay of thirty days (but this last order is very rarely made).[22]

In all security cases, the written order withholding the visit can be challenged in the High Court. According to the Association for Civil Rights in Israel, once the petition challenging the order has been filed, the GSS often back down and allow the lawyer to visit, so that the hearing becomes unnecessary.

Extension of detention hearings

A detainee from the West Bank or Gaza must be brought before the court within eighteen days of her arrest.[23] Under Israeli law the detainee must be brought before a court within forty eight hours of her arrest.[24]

Extension of detention hearings are generally a mere formality. If a lawyer represents the detainee, he or she may be forbidden from speaking to her. Sometimes, if the detainee asks to address the court, (for example to complain that she has been tortured), the lawyer will be told to leave the courtroom while she does so. Hanan Rahim, a Palestinian Israeli detained in December 1989 described her first extension of detention hearing thus:

> After forty eight hours, I was taken to Acre Magistrates Court for my detention to be extended. My lawyer was present, but I was forbidden to speak to her. In addition, I was told that I could only address the judge in the absence of my lawyer. I said nothing at all. My lawyer asked why the *Shabak* wanted to extend the detention. The reply was, "in order to interrogate her". They said that forty eight hours had not been sufficient. The judge accepted this, and gave the *Shabak* a further seven days.

The procedure at the hearing is for the representative of the GSS [25] to ask for the detention to be extended by a given period and for the judge to grant the request without more ado. If the defence lawyer queries the necessity of further detention, it is usually sufficient for the representative to say simply that the GSS need further time to interrogate the woman.

It is very rare for an application for extension of detention to be refused. However, sometimes the detainee is able to get some benefit from the hearing. If she has already made a confession, and wants to retract it, she can demand that her retraction be formally entered on the court record. This is important, because when a detainee tells her interrogators that she wishes to retract what she has said, they usually refuse to record this. Secondly, if the woman is in bad condition physically when she appears in court, it is possible for her or her lawyer to insist that this fact be entered on the record. This may be important later should she wish to allege that her confession was obtained as a result of abuse. Sometimes the judge will order that the woman be seen by a doctor, or even make this a condition of his extending the detention. (It does not follow, however, that the GSS will comply with this order. See below, "Access to Medical Care".) The court usually extends the detention by fifteen or sometimes thirty days. Forty-five days is the longest initial extension possible, and would be granted in a case where the allegation was very serious.

Once the period of the extension has expired, the GSS can seek a further extension (up to a maximum total of six months) to continue the interrogation. When the interrogation has been completed, if the detainee is charged, she will be taken to court, and at this stage the detention can be extended until the end of her trial. The detainee now leaves the GSS section and is placed either in the main part of the detention centre or transferred to a prison.[26]

Sometimes a detainee is released without charge, for example if she did not confess and the GSS have no other evidence on the basis of which to prosecute her; or if the purpose of the interrogation was information-gathering only.

Visits by the International Committee of the Red Cross

The International Committee of the Red Cross and the Israeli government have a bilateral agreement, under which the Israeli authorities are obliged to notify the ICRC of the whereabouts of detainees from the Occupied Territories within twelve days of the arrest, and to permit an ICRC representative to visit the detainee within fourteen days of arrest. At the beginning of the *intifada*, with the large number of arrests, the Israelis did not honour this agreement and the ICRC found it necessary to institute its own system for tracing prisoners. The army eventually began to record names of detainees on a computer. At present, the ICRC is generally informed of new arrests according to the time scale in the agreement. However, a period of twelve days before the ICRC have to be notified of the whereabouts of the detainee is far too long.

There are severe restrictions on what ICRC representatives can do to help detainees. They cannot advise a detainee of her right to consult a lawyer and they cannot pass on any information they obtain from the detainee to any individual or body except the Israeli authorities. They can request that the detainee be examined by an ICRC doctor, but again, the doctor's report may be passed only to the Israeli authorities. Occasionally, the ICRC issue press releases indicating, in very general terms, that they are concerned about the treatment of detainees in interrogation.[27]

Informing Family of the Arrest

In practice, the authorities are extremely lax about informing relatives of arrests and of where detainees are being held. In the Occupied Territories, relatives often learn of an arrest by word of mouth, for example when somebody is released and comes to inform a family that their son is in prison, or when a lawyer visits a prison to see one detainee and discovers by chance that someone else is also being held in that prison. This often happens with male detainees. Since women are more often arrested from their homes than from the street, the family is likely to be aware of the arrest itself. The problem then is to discover where the woman is being held, although this too is easier than with a male detainee as there are fewer detention centres with facilities for women. While the authorities fail in their obligation to inform the family, a persistent lawyer is usually able to obtain the information by telephoning the Legal Adviser in the Civil Administration offices.

The law on informing the family of the detention, for residents of the West Bank and Gaza, is as follows. By Military Order,[28] a detainee's next-of-kin shall be informed without delay of his arrest and whereabouts. However, if the person is suspected of an offence carrying a sentence of more than three years, a judge may permit the announcement of the arrest to be delayed for a period of up to ninety-six hours, which may be extended to allow a sum total of eight days.[29]

Visits by Relatives

Family visits to women under interrogation are never allowed.

Bail and Charge

Bail applications are very rarely successful and some lawyers no longer bother to make them. It is usual for a detainee who is charged following interrogation to remain in custody until her trial is heard. Two of the women interviewed for this report were granted bail.

The law requires that a security detainee from the West Bank or Gaza be charged or released within six months of the date of arrest. Security detainees held under Israeli law must be charged within sixty days (or four months if suspected of treason or espionage). A period of interrogation must not exceed these time limits. In practice, few female detainees are interrogated for as long as one and a half months.

Legal Costs

There is no system of public funding for the legal costs of poor detainees. This is a serious problem as many Palestinians detained are people without financial resources, and the frequent delays in the court system cause legal costs to mount up very quickly. However, it seems that detainees rarely go entirely unrepresented for this reason. Some lawyers are willing to reduce their fees or act unpaid in cases of severe hardship.

Access to Medical Care

There are two issues here. Firstly, the right of the sick or injured detainee to medical care *per se*, which is well established in international humanitarian law.[30] Secondly, the right of the detainee to independent medical examination which, were it available, would be the most effective way to establish whether or not physical or psychological abuse were taking place during interrogation.

A detainee from the West Bank or Gaza has a legal right to medical treatment and to a medical report, but the person providing these is a member of the prison staff and does not have to be a registered doctor.[31] The position is similar under Israeli law. There is no right to independent medical examination for detainees, either for those from the West Bank or Gaza or those tried under Israeli law. In practice, it is almost never permitted. In one rare case documented in this report where an independent doctor was permitted to examine a prisoner shortly after her interrogation had ended, permission was not granted until the detainee's greatest need for him had passed.[32]

In practice, medical care is treated as a privilege, to be provided at the discretion of the commander of the detention centre. Many women report having been refused medical care whilst under interrogation, sometimes in circumstances where they believed their lives to be in danger. Salwa

Abu Hani, from Jerusalem, became very ill during her detention in October 1987, and medical care was seriously delayed.

She describes her second extension of detention hearing, at Haifa Magistrates court:

> By this time I was so weak from the *shabah* [33] and lack of food and sleep, that I could not walk or speak. I was also ill from my stomach ulcers, and I had a high fever. I really felt as if I was going to die. I was carried into the court room on a stretcher. I was then held upright by GSS officers. At one point, they loosened their grip on me with the result that I fell down the flight of steps leading to the cells. I sustained a cut to the head and bruises. An Arab Member of Knesset, Muhammad Mi'ari happened to be in the court room when I arrived. He could see the condition I was in. ...[he] addressed the court on my behalf, demanding that I should be examined by an Arab doctor and asking that I be released on bail. The judge appeared to be shocked by my appearance. He ordered that a prison doctor [an Israeli] be brought to me immediately. However, he extended my detention...
>
> Three days after the court appearance, a doctor came to see me. He asked me about my stomach ulcers. A prison officer was present, and the doctor said to him in Hebrew "this is a serious case". I understand Hebrew. The prison officer told the doctor not to speak Hebrew in front of me. The doctor then turned to me and told me, in English, that my condition was not serious. He said that I was simply suffering because of my stomach ulcers and my leg muscles were tired from the *shabah*.

When medical care is provided, it is invariably inadequate. Inexperienced nurses are often the only personnel available, and sometimes doctors who do not speak Arabic. The detainee is then obliged to rely on a police officer's translation of the doctor's diagnosis. Akamol (like Paracetamol) is prescribed for most complaints.

Notes

1. A high percentage of detainees are released without charge. The Landau Commission Report (see Chapter Four) puts the figure at 50%, and quotes the General Security Services as making a deliberate policy of interrogating many detainees purely as an information gathering exercise.
2. In some cases, the Israelis use 'administrative detention' as an alternative to criminal proceedings. This power is available both in military law in the West Bank and Gaza and in Israeli law. An order is made for the person to be detained without trial or charge, for a period of either six months or a year. It is used when the authorities have no evidence with which to secure a conviction, or where they wish to keep secret the evidence they do have.

3. These figures were supplied by al-Haq, the Palestinian human rights organization affiliated to the International Commission of Jurists. The figure of 79,000 includes approximately 14,000 who were placed in administrative detention.
4. Nineteen women have been administratively detained during the *intifada.*
5. The term 'detainee' is used throughout the report to refer to a person under interrogation; 'defendant' refers to a person facing trial.
6. International humanitarian law permits an occupying power to promulgate laws aimed at protecting its security forces and to set up military courts empowered to try offences against these laws: Fourth Geneva Convention 1949, Articles 64 & 66 (see Appendix I); however, the jurisdiction of the Israeli military courts goes far beyond what is permitted.
7. Military Order 101 of 1967.
8. Military Order 378 of 1970.
9. *Inquiry into the Israeli Military Court System in the Occupied West Bank and Gaza, Report of a Mission,* J.J. Paust, G.von Glahn and G. Woratsch, International Commission of Jurists, December 1989.
10. Israel purported to annex East Jerusalem in 1967, although the annexation was not accepted by the international community. Palestinians resident there have the legal status of "permanent Israeli residents". For the purposes of criminal and security law, they are treated like Israelis.
11. Military charges are brought under the British Defence (Emergency) Regulations of 1945, which the Israeli authorities regard as still being in force, although the British claim to have repealed them at the end of the Mandate.
12. Suggested reading on the operation of the military courts: Chapter 6 in al-Haq Annual Report 1989 *A Nation Under Siege; Inquiry into the Israeli Military Court System in the Occupied West Bank and Gaza, Report of a Mission* by the International Commission of Jurists 1989 (see footnote 9 above); *Justice? The Military Court System in the Israeli-Occupied Territories,* a joint report by al-Haq and the Gaza Centre for Rights and Law, February 1987.
13. The police deal with people who are arrested for minor offences and are not interrogated.
14. The inaccuracy of the official position is symptomatic of the obstruction which members of the public encounter when they try to obtain information on the operation of the GSS.
15. Recently a new system has been set up whereby some complaints against the police are investigated by an office in the Ministry of Justice – ie an office independent of the Ministry of Police.
16. Obviously the accountability referred to is to the Israeli electorate, and Palestinians from the Occupied Territories can benefit from it only indirectly.
17. Lawyers hold differing views on which body it is most effective to address the complaint to.

18. The holding of Palestinian residents of the Occupied Territories in centres inside Israel is a violation of Article 76 of the Fourth Geneva Convention 1949 – see Appendix I.
19. This is one of the problems with making complaints via the commander of the detention centre, who is a police officer.
20. This is in breach of Article 72 of the Fourth Geneva Convention – see Appendix I.
21. See Military Order 1220, Amendment no.53, which amends Military Order 378 of 1970 for the West Bank. The rules for Gazans appear in a different Military Order but they are the same. MO 1220 was issued in March 1988.
22. Section 29, Criminal Procedure Law.
23. The rule for Gaza is in an unnumbered Military Order of 1970; the West Bank rule number has not been located; it is probably Military Order 378.
24. Penal Law 1977 section 125.
25. The GSS are represented by the military prosecutor in the West Bank and Gaza, or the police in Israel. GSS personnel do not appear at these hearings.
26. Palestinian women from the Occupied Territories are usually held in Tel Mond prison, near Tel Aviv, and Palestinian women from Israel as well as Jewish Israeli women are held in Neve Tirza prison, near Ramla.
27. For example, on 16 July 1991 the ICRC issued a press release announcing that it had "today submitted a further report to the highest authorities of the State of Israel, on the situation of detainees undergoing interrogation in Israel and the Occupied Territories". After remarking that numerous such reports have been sent to the Israeli authorities with the aim of improving the treatment of detainees, the release went on:
"The ICRC appeals to the Israeli authorities to give special attention to the treatment of detainees under interrogation, and to implement the recommendations it has already made." (See also Chapter Four, under the heading "Systematic Torture".
28. Military Order 1220, Amendment number 53, Article 78a(b). See also footnote 21 above.
29. Ibid Article 78d(a) 1 & 2.
30. Article 76, Fourth Geneva Convention 1949, see Appendix I.
31. Military Order 29(5) in the West Bank and Military Order 410(5) in Gaza.
32. The case of Na'ila 'Ayish, who miscarried while in interrogation: see Chapter Two, "Case Study" and Appendix IV.
33. *Shabah* means being left shackled in an awkward position, often squatting, for a prolonged period – see Chapter Two.

Chapter Two
Methods of Interrogation

> *[A]ny act by which severe pain or suffering, whether physical or mental, is intentionally inflicted on a person for such purposes as obtaining from him or a third person information or a confession, punishing him for an act he or a third person has committed or is suspected of having committed, or intimidating or coercing him or a third person, or for any reason based on discrimination of any kind, when such pain or suffering is inflicted by or at the instigation of or with the consent or acquiescence of a public official or other person acting in an official capacity. It does not include pain or suffering arising only from, inherent in or incidental to, lawful sanctions.*

Article One of The United Nations Convention Against Torture and other Cruel, Inhuman or Degrading Treatment or Punishment, 1984.

The process of trying to make the detainee confess begins at the moment of arrest. Many of the same methods are used with detainees of both sexes. However, the GSS have developed certain techniques specifically for women. These include sexual harassment, manipulation of the Arab notion of 'female honour' and manipulation of mothers' concern about their children. The methods which are specific to women will be given the most thorough consideration.

Arrest and Transportation

Whether she is arrested by GSS officers, police or soldiers, the woman defendant is likely to be subjected to sexual harassment from the first moment. Women are most commonly arrested from their homes, but sometimes in the street or for example on a demonstration. During the journey from the place of arrest to the initial place of detention, the female detainee is likely to be called a 'prostitute', 'whore' and other insulting names. Comments may be made about her body and she may be threatened with rape. She may also be beaten, kicked or spat at.

Suha Sanduqa, a Jerusalem resident, was arrested at age 14 outside Damascus Gate in Jerusalem, on suspicion of swearing at a police officer. This was in June 1989. She was taken to the Qishlah police station in the Old City.

> On the way to the Qishlah, I was beaten in the police car by a policeman using a truncheon. This was repeated on arrival at the Qishlah. I was struck on my left arm and my left leg.

Suha was arrested again in February 1990, as she was leaving school. She was now fifteen. This time she was accused of throwing a stone at an Egged bus.

> I was put in a car and driven to the Russian Compound. In the car, one of the two men spat at me. I was also slapped on my face.

The woman may be taken directly to an interrogation centre, or she may be taken initially to a police station, military post or local prison and then later transferred to the interrogation centre. This will depend on the place and circumstances of the arrest. All of these venues are staffed largely by men, and she may be subjected to further harassment along the way. Usually, once the woman reaches the interrogation centre, she remains there throughout her interrogation. In a few cases, women have been transferred several times during the interrogation, from one centre to another, presumably in order to disorientate them.

Arrival at the GSS Section

A police woman or female soldier may be present at the arrest, and during the journeys, again depending on the circumstances. The law requires that when a female detainee arrives at the interrogation centre, a female soldier or police officer carries out certain procedures, such as the body search.[1] However, by the time the woman is taken to the GSS section of the centre, she is likely to be alone in the custody of men.

As explained above, the GSS have their own sections in each of the facilities where women are interrogated and these sections are effectively under their exclusive control.

By this stage, the woman may have been given some indication of the reason for her arrest.[2] Detailed questioning does not usually begin until the woman is taken into the first interrogation session. However, she may be informally questioned from the moment of arrest onwards. In cases where the detainee is a known activist, the GSS officers who are to interrogate her may have accompanied the police who arrested the woman, and questioning may have begun on the journey from her home to the interrogation centre.

Most women other than the very young would be aware that the fact that they are being taken to the GSS section means that they are going to be interrogated.[3]

In most cases, even if it is her first experience of detention, the woman will be aware that once she is taken to the GSS section she faces the possibility of being held there for a long time in complete isolation. She will know that she could be held for days or even weeks without being able to contact her family and children, without seeing a lawyer, without receiving medical care should she need it and without being taken to court. The vast numbers of Palestinian men who have been arrested since the start of the *intifada*, and the general level of political awareness, ensure that most Palestinian women have heard accounts of interrogation experiences. Women who are politically active may have a detailed knowledge of what to expect; this however is not typical. A village woman from a remote part of the West Bank, on the other hand, may be completely ignorant of what she faces.

Sleep, Food and Hygiene Deprivation

The standard GSS practice during the first few days of interrogation is to try to destroy the detainee's physical well being. She will be prevented from sleeping and efforts will be made to disorientate her. A foul-smelling sack will usually be placed over her head when she is transferred from one part of the GSS section to another. She may be interrogated in the middle of the night, and in between sessions she may be held in darkness, or in an artificially lit cell, so that she loses all sense of time.

Fatma Salama, a 28 year old woman from Nablus, described the beginning of her detention as follows:

> I was arrested... on July 25 1990 at 10.15 in the evening. They took me to the Shin Bet and Police Centre in Nablus... I stayed on a chair all night long until 9am. Then they handcuffed me and transferred me to Jalama. When we arrived at Jalama they placed a black sack on my head and made me sit on the stairs for such a long time that I cannot remember how long it was. Then they took me into interrogation, where there were three interrogators... I was already tired when they arrested me at home as I had my period, which affects me a lot.

Fatma Abu Bakra, from Gaza, now in her thirties, described more long term sleep deprivation:

> I was arrested on 23 November 1986. After a day or two in Gaza, I was sent to Ashkelon and interrogated there. First, they prevented me from sleeping for four or five days. All that time I was sitting on a chair. Early in the morning, they let me sit on the floor, but not sleep.

During the first few days, there are likely to be at least two interrogation sessions in each twenty four hours, each one lasting for several hours. In between interrogation sessions, the detainee may be placed in *shabah* or in the 'coffin'. Both of these make sleep impossible. *Shabah* means that the detainee is made to squat, stand with legs bent, or sit, handcuffed to the wall of an outdoor yard. The 'coffin' is a tiny closet, measuring about one metre square, into which the detainee is locked for hours at a time. Both will be described in more detail below.

Maha Nassar, a 36 year old mother of two from Jerusalem, was arrested on 4 October 1989. This was her fifth detention. GSS officers came to her house at 2.30 am and took her directly to the Russian Compound. After a half hour interrogation she was placed in a *zinzana* or tiny cell. (This cell usually measures about one and a half metres by two metres. It is different from the 'coffin'). Two hours later she was interrogated again briefly. Then, at about 7am:

> This time I was taken to the yard... and placed in *shabah*. I was hooded... For the next four days, in between interrogation sessions, I was in *shabah* continuously. I was not taken to the cells at all.

Sometimes the woman is placed in a cell on arrival, and in between interrogation sessions. It is almost always a tiny, filthy *zinzana*. At best there will be a very thin foam mattress on the floor and a hole for a toilet. There is unlikely to be a supply of water. Descriptions given by detainees suggest that the conditions vary from centre to centre and from detainee to detainee. Ra'ida Al'Ataba, a 23 year old woman from Nablus, said:

> When we arrived at Jalama they immediately put us into a *zinzana* which was in horrible condition. There were cockroaches and dirt in it.

Roni Ben Efrat is a Jewish Israeli journalist and peace activist; she was arrested on 24 April 1988 and detained in the GSS section of Petakh Tikva police station.

> On the first night I was placed in a cell measuring one and a half by two metres. It was filthy. I was given a dirty mattress and three stinking blankets. There was a hole in the floor for a toilet, which was blocked. There was no tap. The whole cell smelled very bad... I complained about the toilet hole in my cell being blocked. After three days I was moved to a new cell. Here the hole was not blocked but the light did not work and the walls appeared to be smeared with faeces. I remained in that cell, without light, for eight days. When I asked to be allowed to clean the cell, permission was denied. I was eventually moved to a cell with a light that worked.

Hanan Rahim, a 30 year old Palestinian Israeli from the Galilee, was arrested on 17 December 1989.

> In Jalama I was taken to the women's section, to a small cell measuring about two metres by one and a half metres. There were two windows, which were kept open all the time. The weather was very cold and there was no heating in the cell. The cell had a mattress, a toilet and a basin with a tap from which I drank.

During the early days of interrogation, the detainee is likely to be deprived of food and sometimes water. In the hot summer months, this can be life-threatening. If food is provided, it is usually dirty, unappetizing and

"Women in a village near Hebron gather outside the house of one of three martyrs who have just been killed, during the imposition of a curfew by the army. The occasion is the second anniversary of the outbreak of the *intifada.*"

Photographer: *Nadia Sultani*

insufficient in quantity. Sometimes access to a toilet is denied, and usually the woman is not allowed to wash or to change her clothes. Menstruating women are almost never provided with sanitary protection.

Maha Nassar, who spent her first four days in *shabah*, was given no food during that time, and water only infrequently. When at last food was offered, she decided to go on hunger strike.

> After four days of starvation, I was offered food. By this time, my stomach was in a bad way. I decided to refuse the food and go on hunger strike. The interrogators asked me when I was going to accept food. I replied that I would eat when they took me out of this dirty place. In all I did not eat for thirteen days, although I drank water occasionally. I lost 10kgs.

Salwa Abu Hani, a 29 year old woman from the West Bank, was arrested on 27 September 1987 and taken to Jalama. For the first seven days she was put in *shabah* between interrogation sessions.

> I was given water from the start of my interrogation, but was denied food altogether for the first five days. As a result of this treatment, my stomach ulcers began to cause me problems and I quickly became very sick.

At a later stage in her interrogation, Salwa was held in a *zinzana*. There were no toilet facilities, and when she asked to be taken out to use the toilet, this was refused. She was obliged to soil herself. She was also refused a shower.

Iman Jadallah, a 27 year old woman from Jerusalem, was arrested on 24 July 1990 and taken to the Russian Compound. During the next ten days she was held in the interrogation room, both during and in between sessions. At night she was tied to a chair while the interrogators slept. She says:

> I demanded a number of times to go to the toilet but my demand was rejected; I felt severe pain in the kidney area.

Many women describe being refused permission to wash or shower.

Maryam Qadumi, a 19 year old Palestinian Israeli who was interrogated in Jalama in June 1990, says:

> There was no shower in the cell. During the thirteen days of my detention I frequently asked to be allowed to take a shower, but was always refused. I was unable to change my clothes throughout.

Terry Boullata, from Jerusalem, was arrested on 4 November 1987, when she was 21. She was interrogated in the Russian Compound.

> I had now been under interrogation for thirteen days and had not been allowed to wash. I began shouting loudly, demanding to be allowed to take a shower. After a long time they agreed to this. They

> turned on the water in my cell, which was a very light trickle of very hot water. It fell over the "toilet" hole in the floor of the cell. In order to wash myself I was obliged to use a plastic yogurt container which normally I used to drink tea from. It took a long time for the yogurt pot to fill up with the drips of water, so that I could wash my hair and myself. The whole shower must have taken an hour. I was then allowed to change into some clean clothes which had been brought to the Russian Compound for me.

In Terry's case, although the shower and change of clothes were permitted, they were used as an opportunity to increase the physical pressure she was under. She goes on:

> However, before I was able to put on my coat, the guards came and took me out to the yard and put me in *shabah*. It was night time, and after the very hot water I felt the cold terribly.

Michal Schwartz, a 41 year old Jewish Israeli journalist and peace activist was arrested on 27 April 1988 and interrogated at Petakh Tikva police station at the same time as Roni Ben Efrat. Both women were allowed to take showers after an initial refusal.

> I was refused permission to wash or shower for the first three days, and was then given a shower every one or two days (although this was occasionally refused as a punishment).

The denial of washing facilities is part of a process of destroying the woman's morale. Hooding the detainee also contributes to this. Ra'ida Al'Ataba described it thus:

> Usually when I was taken to interrogation they would put a black sack on my head before I entered interrogation. The sack would remain on my head for a long time, until I was soaked with sweat. Then they would take me into the interrogation room.

Sometimes women are handcuffed as well as hooded. Maryam Qadumi:

> Every time I was taken out of this cell a sack was placed over my head and I was handcuffed. Usually the sack was left on until the interrogators were ready to start questioning me, and then it was removed. Sometimes the handcuffs were left on during the interrogation session, other times they were removed.

Physical Abuse and Sensory Deprivation: Beatings, *Shabah*, Exposure to Heat and Cold, Threat of Electric Shock, the 'Coffin'

While her strength is decreasing due to deprivation of sleep, food and hygiene, the Palestinian woman detainee is likely also to be subjected to immediate physical pain (or put in fear of it). In this important respect, the Jewish Israeli women interviewed were treated quite differently from Palestinian women (whether from the Occupied Territories or inside Israel). The Israeli women were assured by the GSS, shortly after their arrests, that they would not be subjected to physical pressure, and this promise was kept.

The GSS feel no taboo against using physical violence against Palestinian women. It is not common for the violence to be such as to cause very serious long-term injuries. No woman has yet died while under interrogation [4] and reports of broken bones or internal injuries are rare. There are, however, cases of pregnant detainees who miscarried during interrogation, and several of the women interviewed described quite serious muscle damage which they attributed to long periods in *shabah*. The GSS are very careful to ensure that detainees are not released with visible physical injuries, which makes it very difficult to prove that abuse has taken place.

Male detainees are regularly subjected to most of the same forms of physical abuse as women. However, it is important to remember that, throughout her time in the hands of the GSS, the female detainee is made to feel sexually threatened. Many women detainees report having been threatened with rape. This adds an extra dimension of fear to the experience of physical abuse.

Beatings

Women are routinely slapped, and kicked during interrogation sessions if they do not readily answer questions. Sometimes an interrogator will bang the woman's head against the wall. Maryam Qadumi describes her second interrogation session:

> About 6.30pm I was taken for another interrogation session. The same interrogators were present. One of them continued to ask me about membership in an illegal organization. When I refused to answer his questions, he aimed a kick at me. His foot hit the chair I was sitting on. He also slapped my face every time I refused to answer.

The following evening she was interrogated again:

> When I refused to speak, they slapped my face. One of the interrogators used to sit directly in front of me, very close, and would spit in my face. He placed his feet on top of my feet, resting them there; when I refused to speak, he would apply pressure.

As the hours went by, Maryam found it harder to withstand the continuous violence. The next morning:

> I was shown a photograph of a demonstration and asked to sign a statement to the effect that I was present. I did not want to do so. However, one of the interrogators hit me in the stomach, and because of that I signed the statement.

Fatma Abu Bakra (above) was subjected to very serious sexual harassment during her interrogation in Ashkelon in 1986. Before this began, she was hit on the head and throttled.

> I was beaten on my head. The name of my interrogator was "Steve". "Steve" would strangle me. He was tall and held me from the back so my legs would not touch the floor. He would put his fingers on my throat and when I gasped for breath he would release me and look at his watch. This happened four or five times a day for three days.

Many women report that each interrogator would take on a specific role during the sessions. Thus it may be only one of three or four interrogators who actually strike the detainee, while another verbally abuses her and a third plays the 'nice guy' who wants to 'help' her. Na'ila 'Ayish, from Gaza, was arrested in February 1987 when she was a few weeks pregnant.[5] She describes an interrogation session:

> The interrogators cursed me and threatened to undress me. One of them... slammed my head against the wall... I felt like an object of play – as if they divided roles among themselves: One would curse me, one would hit, one pretended he wanted to help.

Unlike the other forms of physical abuse discussed later in this section, beatings usually occur during the actual interrogation sessions. After the detainee has been struck once, she is constantly aware that this may be repeated at any moment. This contributes to the atmosphere of tension and fear in which she is answering questions (or trying to exercise her right to silence). It is important to remember that, as time goes on, she will be in an increasingly weak physical state.

Shabah and extremes of Heat and Cold

Shabah, also known as 'Palestinian hanging', was referred to above. Its use is very common for both male and female detainees. Terry Boullata describes her experience of it in November 1987.

> At night I was regularly taken to the yard for *shabah*. I would be made to perch on a low concrete ledge which projected from the wall, with my hands tied behind me to a metal bar. There was a metal spike sticking out of the wall so that I could not straighten my back. A foul smelling sack was placed over my head.

Women are placed in *shabah* in many different positions: Standing, often with legs shackled wide apart (probably intended to accentuate the woman's consciousness of her vulnerability to rape); standing on one leg; perching on a ledge as described above; sitting.

Detainees are usually placed in an outdoor yard for *shabah*, so that they will be exposed to the weather. In summer there is no protection from extreme heat and in winter there is no protection from the cold and rain. For example, the pregnant Na'ila 'Ayish was made to spend three nights outdoors in *shabah* in the rain during her interrogation in February 1987.

In the Russian Compound in Jerusalem, both male and female detainees are placed in the same yard for *shabah*. Each detainee is shackled and hooded, so there is no possibility of communication. It appears that the intention is to make the detainee feel dehumanized and isolated, as well as causing him or her acute physical discomfort. Maha Nassar describes her feelings on catching a glimpse of men in *shabah* when she was being taken to an interrogation session and the guard had forgotten to hood her.

> On the way to the interrogation room I was taken through a small glass doorway into a yard. I saw about twenty men who were in *shabah* around the walls of the yard. It was the first time that I saw the yard as it really was. It made me feel very bad to see the men, you know, I was seeing part of my people who were suffering. I could not see their faces – I thought, maybe one of them is my brother, maybe one of them is my neighbour – nobody knows – but I do know that these are people who have their lives, who have their children, who have their past, their future... What are they thinking of? they are just, you know, ghosts around the wall.

Exposure to extremes of heat and cold is another tactic used to cause the detainee physical discomfort. Terry Boullata said:

> I was often left alone in the interrogation room for long periods. I would be left sitting with my hands behind my back manacled to the chair, placed in front of the air conditioning which was turned down to the coldest temperature. It was November and as a result of this I suffered pains in my chest.

Hanan Rahim describes similar treatment during her December 1989 interrogation:

> At 7am a prison officer came to take me to another room. I was handcuffed and hooded. On arrival I was placed in front of an air conditioning vent and the hood was removed. The air was on hot for half an hour, and then cold for half an hour. The cold air was very cold, and I jumped up and down to keep warm.

Threat of Electric Shock

One of the women interviewed said that she was threatened with being subjected to electric shock. She says that she was actually strapped into a special chair and the controller appeared to be about to turn the current on, when the interrogator in charge relented. This was in Jalama detention centre. Nineteen year old Maryam Qadumi said:

> From the beginning of my interrogation, the *Shabak* [6] had threatened me with electric shocks. On the sixth day of my interrogation,

> Wednesday June 20 1990, they were asking me questions and I was refusing to talk. They took me to a room with a red light and a special chair. The chair was made of iron and leather and had wires attached to it. I was made to sit in it and a prison officer connected the wires to my arms and legs. I was extremely frightened. The interrogator who was in charge told the prison officer to turn on the current. Then, seconds later, he told the prison officer to wait. He said he wanted me to have time to think about whether or not I now wanted to confess. Meanwhile, I had said nothing. I was taken out of the chair and back to the tiny cell. I was told to think again about whether I wanted to confess. If I would not, they would bring me back to the electric shock room and this time they would turn on the current.
>
> In fact I was left in the tiny cell for a couple of hours and then taken back to the interrogation room. I did not confess and I was not taken to the electric shock room again. The interrogation continued as before.

Reports of the use of electric shock on male detainees have been made.[7] Another of the women interviewed for this report, Hanan Rahim, described a youth whom she knew being brought into the room where she was being interrogated. He was very pale and had difficulty standing. She was told by the GSS that he had been subjected to electric shock. When she met him after both of them had been released, he confirmed this.

The 'Coffin'

Many women describe being locked into a tiny, claustrophobic, dark closet for hours at a time, in between interrogation sessions. This is a sensory deprivation device aimed at severely disorientating the detainee. Ex-detainees have nicknamed it variously the 'coffin', the 'grave' and the 'cupboard' (*khazana* in Arabic).

The coffin measures about one metre square and is two metres high. It is deliberately kept in a state of filth and women report having difficulty breathing in it due to lack of ventilation.

Iman Jadallah, a 27 year old civil engineer from Jerusalem arrested on 24 July 1990, describes being put in the coffin on the second day of her detention in the Russian Compound:

> When I denied all the charges they told me that they would take me to a "hotel". Actually I was brought to this "hotel", which is a one square metre closet, two metres high, dark and without any opening. I remained there for several days, during which I was brought to interrogation and returned to the "hotel"...

Throughout the first four days of her interrogation in July 1988, Maha Nassar (see above) was held in the 'coffin' in between interrogation sessions. She was fed infrequently and was only allowed to go to the toilet on the way to the interrogation room. She describes both the physical discomfort and the psychological effects of being in the coffin:

You feel isolated throughout your time in the *Shabak* section of the prison. In the coffin you feel really isolated because it has two locked doors. You step through the first door, then after two or three steps you have another door and then you enter the tiny room. It measures about one metre by one metre. You cannot lie down, you have to stand or squat. If you want to stretch your legs, there are two stone steps at waist height, on the walls facing each other. You have to sit on one step and stretch your leg out with your foot placed on the other step.

Of course you don't have a toilet inside and it is very very dark. There is a very thin hole high up on the wall, from which they suck out the air, for ventilation otherwise the prisoner would die of lack of oxygen. I had some trouble breathing.

I could hear sounds from inside the coffin. There was a slow knocking sound which seemed to come from a very deep place inside the wall. There was a sound of a snake hissing and the sound of deep crying. I heard sounds like that, for a long time.

This experience of the coffin is intended to destroy the prisoner from inside. You feel that you are very far from all of your family and from all of your friends, a place where you are at the mercy of two or three Shin Bet officers who have ugly faces and an ugly way of treating people.

After four days in the coffin, I was taken to the isolation cells...

People who are well-informed before they go into detention know what to expect and I think it is the will that is tested in there, not the body. It is not a question of how much you can bear physically, but of how strong you are mentally.[8]

Drugging

In August 1990, a woman alleged that she had made a confession under the influence of a drug administered to her while in the GSS section of the Russian Compound. Iman Jadallah swore an affidavit to this effect in the presence of her lawyer when the latter was permitted to visit her during the interrogation period. The information given is based on the affidavit and on a press release by Sanabel Press Services on 7 August 1990.

After ten days Iman Jadallah was taken to a solitary confinement cell. A "prisoner" in the cell next to hers spoke with her through a pipe, claiming to be a member of the political organization about which she was being interrogated and otherwise sympathizing with her. He told her that another "prisoner" would soon appear in the corridor, that the "prisoner" was sympathetic and that she could ask him for anything she needed.

Later the second "prisoner" did in fact appear, passed in front of her cell several times and offered to bring her anything she needed, including a hot cup of tea. She accepted the tea. After Jadallah drank the tea she began to feel dizzy and that her head was extremely heavy. Her heartbeat became erratic, strong and painful. She felt unable to control herself; when she stood up her legs felt like "cotton"; she bumped into the walls, including bumping her head.

The "prisoner" who had been passing back and forth then gave her small pieces of paper and told her to write anything she wanted on them. She began writing notes as he asked questions. Five minutes later she was summoned to interrogation, where she was given a large sheet of paper. According to Jadallah she was unable to control herself or to think about anything; she began writing a 'confession'. When she finished she was forced, by means of the same threats that had been used during the first ten days [9], to add two more sentences to what she had written. Two hours after she drank the tea a rash appeared on Jadallah's face.[10]

The next day, August 3rd, she was taken to her home and to various locations in the village which she pointed out to the GSS and soldiers. According to Jadallah, when she found herself showing the soldiers the locations she began to "wake up" and to feel that she had been saying and doing things beyond her control.

Sexual harassment

While the detainee is becoming progressively weaker from the combination of sleep and food deprivation with physical abuse, she must also cope with a barrage of verbal sexual taunts, threats and in some cases, actual assault. Generally, these occur during interrogation sessions.

Hanan Rahim described her first interrogation session in Jalama Detention Centre as follows. It was her first arrest.

> The interrogator who was doing most of the talking kept insulting me, using sexual words and innuendo. He told me to look him in the eye as he spoke to me, but I avoided his gaze. Various threats were made to me. They said that they would rape me; that they would put me in another room and bring a Druze man to rape me; that they would kill me. They also said that they would put me with collaborators, and that, since there were no women collaborators available, they would put me in a room with male collaborators.

The number of interrogators in each session varies, usually between about two and six. All the interrogators are male. The detainee is acutely aware that she is in their sole custody – there is nobody for her to complain to, or to seek protection from.

By law, a woman is required to be present during all interrogation sessions of women detainees. In practice the rule is often broken.[11] The majority of the Palestinian women interviewed for this report said that no woman was present during their interrogation sessions. Those who had a woman present say that she did not intervene to protect them from sexual or other forms of harassment, and in some cases the woman was asked to, and did, leave the room when the interrogators wanted to use more extreme forms of abuse.

One woman said:

> A woman clerk was present during 90% of my interrogation sessions. The *Shabak* told me that her role was to protect my honour as an Arab woman. However, despite the way I was treated, the woman never spoke or did anything at all. (Hanan Rahim)

Another recounted:

> During the interrogation there was a woman in the room. Every time they wanted to hit or torture me, they took me to another room. (Fatma Abu Bakra)

All the women interviewed, including the Jewish women, described sexual harassment of one form or another by their interrogators. The severity of the harassment varied, as did the reactions to it of individual women.

It is impossible to measure objectively the severity of instances of sexual harassment. The impact of a sexual threat is conditioned by many factors, both objective and subjective. The former include the context in which the threat is uttered, including the number of people present, the demeanour of the man making the threats and the response of his companions (eg laughter or grim silence); whether the detainee is handcuffed and hooded, how she is dressed, the position in which she is standing or sitting; the proximity to her of the threatener; and, very importantly, whether the threat is accompanied by physical violence of any sort. It hardly needs to be said that the impact on different women of a given act of sexual harassment will vary, depending on such things as the woman's social background, her personality and her personal history.

One important factor likely to influence the subjective reaction of the individual woman is the sexual culture in which she has grown up. The women interviewed for this report come from different communities with differing sexual cultures. Social attitudes to female sexuality are very difficult to assess, however, and, as a foreigner, the author of this report is not well equipped for the task.

In traditional Palestinian society, a woman's "honour", particularly her reputation for sexual innocence, is seen as one of her most important attributes. An insult to (or, worse, a violation of) her honour is a calamity not only for her but also for her family. If she is single, it may affect her marriage prospects.

The role of Palestinian women in the Occupied Territories began to change during the early years of the *intifada*. Women acquired more freedom than they had previously, and, at the same time, social attitudes began to change. To some extent, the upsurge in Islamic fundamentalism which has characterized the second half of the *intifada* has put a check on this process. Nevertheless, it is true to say that whereas, in the early days of the *intifada*, a woman who was sexually harassed by the security forces or the GSS might be blamed for this occurrence, by 1990 she had a chance of being honoured for having survived the ordeal with dignity.

The attitudes of the woman's family and community will depend on a variety of factors, including how religious they are, how traditional, their social class and where their political affiliations lie. In addition there is a marked difference in attitudes between rural people and town dwellers, the former being more traditional in outlook.

It is outside the scope of this report to try to gauge the level of personal and social damage done to women detainees by sexual harassment. However it is worth noting which of the three groups of women whose cases are documented seem to be subjected to the most severe harassment.

Palestinian detainees seem to be subjected to more aggressive sexual harassment than are Jewish Israeli peace activists.[12] This may be partly because the GSS believe that it is more likely to cause distress to Palestinian detainees than it would to the latter. Another reason may be that GSS interrogators feel a certain taboo against sexually harassing Jewish women, which would not operate in their dealings with Palestinian women. No doubt a further restraining factor is the GSS' awareness that Jewish Israeli women are in a much stronger position to seek redress for harassment than are Palestinian women.

In the past, and at the beginning of the *intifada*, women detainees and ex-detainees were often reluctant to talk about the sexual harassment to which they had been subjected, particularly if their lawyer was male (as are the vast majority practising in the military courts). This has changed somewhat (partly thanks to the Israeli Women's Organization for Political Prisoners, which manages to send a woman lawyer into most of the prisons where women are held on remand following their interrogation) although it is highly unlikely that all incidents of serious harassment are now being reported to the lawyer, particularly if the woman is very young or very religious.

The examples that follow are the experiences of women from a variety of backgrounds.

One of the most severe reported cases of sexual harassment and actual assault occurred a year before the beginning of the *intifada*, to Fatma Abu Bakra, a Gazan woman who was being held in Ashkelon. Fatma was interrogated for a period of fifty days, and eventually made a confession. She did not feel able to tell her male lawyers what had happened and it was only when she was visited by a woman lawyer, Leah Tsemel, eleven months later, while on remand, that she first spoke about it. The affidavit taken on that occasion is quoted at some length, because Fatma decided to challenge the admissibility of her confession at trial, on the basis that the confession was made as a result of the sexual harassment (see Chapter Three).[13]

An interrogator calling himself "Abu Allah" took me to another room. I was alone and he played with my face and my b... and said "I want to get ... you now. My hands were not tied so I pushed his face away from me and I started to hit my head against the wall. He ordered me to sit on the floor in the corner. He then sat in front of me on a chair with his legs open. When I pushed his hands away, he used a megaphone to ask another policeman to bring him a special hat with a sponge and handcuffs. Apparently this special hat was to protect my head. He handcuffed my hands behind my back. While he was doing this, I shouted at him that I would expose what he was doing to the entire world. His response was "I will... you and I don't care about you, public opinion, lawyers or the Red Cross". We were still alone in the room. Then he started to play with my b... He put this special hat on my head and went back to sitting the same way while I was in the corner. I screamed all the time and he said, "You have nice b... bitch" and "You must confess now, otherwise we'll transfer you from prison to prison. I'll ... you and we'll all kill you". At that moment a policewoman knocked on the door and he quickly took his hands away from me. She told him something and he said "I'm coming". She left the room and he was still sitting on the chair. He opened my handcuffs and went to the door. The whole time his condition was not normal. I saw his pants were full. He stood with his face to the door and fixed his pants. He left and I was still sitting on the floor.

When he came back, he took me out of the room and interrogated me in the presence of a policewoman. I can't say exactly what day this happened, but it was at night at about 2am. I didn't tell the other interrogators or policewoman about what happened to me because I was afraid of his revenge, especially after he told me that he didn't care about public opinion. I want to say that I was too embarrassed to give details of this event to the male lawyers from Gaza who came to visit me and I still feel embarrassed, but it is easier for me now because you're a woman. I only told the other lawyers that "Abu Allah" did bad things to me.

There was another event that I didn't tell my male lawyers concerning the interrogator "Steve". "Steve" had a picture in his pocket and often when he talked with me, he would take the picture out of his pocket and order me to look at it. I refused and looked away. He then would yell at me and force me to look at it. I saw a picture the size of a cigarette packet, of a man who had a very big ... He told me "That's me when I was young., Look how big my ... was. Now its ten times bigger and I'm going to ... you". He tore at my clothes and I started screaming and hitting my head against the wall. "Abu Allah" and the policewoman were in the room at the time. "Abu Allah" stood between me and "Steve", and "Steve" took off his pants and underwear. I screamed and the policewoman covered her eyes

> with her hands and started laughing. Then he put his pants back on. I don't remember the exact day this all happened but it was one or two days after the event with "Abu Allah". When "Abu Allah" left the room "Steve" began to hit me on the head. All the time the policewoman was present...

Fatma Salama from Nablus describes fairly severe sexual harassment:

> The charge which they accused me of is membership [of a proscribed organization]. When I denied this, they started using dirty language and called me a bitch and said that a million men had slept with me. The interrogators were pushing me off the chair and trying to make me fall on the floor. Then he overturned the chair and demanded that I sit on the overturned chair. I did not agree so he demanded that I take off my clothes. When I told him that I would not take them off he said that he would begin to undress. He actually took off his shirt and started unbuttoning the button of his pants. He said that he was going to undress, that I should undress and that we would get on the table to be photographed so my family would know I was having fun.[14] Of course I attempted not to show that I was severely upset by these actions, although I was exploding inside.
>
> When the interrogator saw that these actions did not shake me, he took off his belt and threatened to beat me. Another took off his shoes and hit me on my face. As for the interrogator [Rami], he said that he would take off his trousers. He said that I was going to kneel in front of him on the floor to suck his sexual organs. Of course I told him that this would not happen... Also during the interrogation, interrogator Rami would put his chair extremely close to the chair I was sitting on. He would open his legs and demand that I also open my legs. Whenever I refused he would pull my legs open by force. I was also wearing a jacket over my blouse in interrogation so he tried to take off the jacket. Also, the zipper of my trousers was not completely zipped up. He told me that I wanted to sleep with him and that this was the reason I unzipped my zipper. I closed the jacket over it so it would not show.

It is important to note that although the interrogators struck Fatma a number of times, the sexual threats made by "Rami" were not carried out. The only directly sexual physical contact he made with her was to pull her legs apart. This is consistent with the type of harassment described by other detainees: with a few notable exceptions, such as Fatma Abu Bakra (above), threats are much more common than actual assault. In this context it is interesting to know how an interrogator in the same institution reacted when another detainee responded to sexual threats by calling his bluff.

Ra'ida al'Ataba, also from Nablus, was interrogated in Jalama on the same day as Fatma Salama, on suspicion of acting for the same organization:

> Two persons began interrogating me... When I did not answer them, [one of the interrogators] put on the black sack again and overturned the chair and said that he was going to make me sit on it while it is overturned. Then he threatened my honour, so I raised my blouse and told him I was not afraid and that he could do whatever he liked. He was angry and started cursing me and describing me as dirty.

The three women quoted above are all from the Occupied Territories. Hanan Rahim, quoted at the beginning of this section, is a Palestinian Israeli. When asked her response to being threatened with rape if she did not confess, she said:

> I did not believe the threats of rape were serious. At one point I was told to remove my clothes, and I refused. Nothing happened.

Another Palestinian Israeli, Maryam Qadumi, describes being frightened initially by sexual harassment.

> I was subjected to a barrage of verbal abuse of a sexual nature. I was called a prostitute and other words which I would rather not repeat. The interrogator also threatened to rape me. Threats of this nature were made throughout the thirteen days of my interrogation. At first I believed that they were meant seriously.

She describes how, the following day, she gradually felt more confident:

> From 10am until 2pm I was interrogated again. During this session, a Palestinian man was brought into the room. I was told that he had made a statement against me, and that, if I did not confess, they would put him in the tiny cell with me and make him rape me. I said that I did not know him. I refused to say anything further.
>
> I was not afraid, since I felt sure that the man would not in fact hurt me. I was feeling better than I had felt the night before. I now had more confidence in my ability to cope with the interrogation.

Salwa Abu Hani, from the West Bank, was subjected to a form of harassment which was both brutal and designed to be particularly humiliating.

> Since I had been breastfeeding prior to my arrest, my breasts were full of milk and consequently very tender. No facilities were provided for me to express the milk. Indeed, one of the interrogators used to come up to me and flick my breasts with his fingers. This was extremely painful. Because of the milk, it felt as if he was punching me with something very hard. I am sure that he was aware of the pain he was causing me.

> On about the third day of the interrogation, I was taken outside to a yard and handcuffed to a chair in front of an air-conditioning vent which was blowing out cold air. My blouse and brassiere were removed. I was left like this for a long time. It was humiliating and very painful. After some time, perhaps an hour and a half, a woman criminal prisoner [an Israeli] must have seen me. I could not see her, but I heard her shouting to the *Shabak* that they must not abuse me like this. They came and brought me back indoors.

The two Jewish Israeli women security detainees who were interviewed for this report were not threatened with rape and were not sexually assaulted. They were, however, subjected to subtle forms of sexual harassment apparently intended to wear away at their nerves and their self esteem.

Michal Schwartz:

> Throughout the interrogation I was made to feel very conscious that I was a woman alone in the hands of men who had a lot of power over me. One would sit very close to me and blow cigarette smoke at me. He would also breathe into my ear for 10 to 15 minutes at a stretch, in an overtly sexual manner. Another interrogator made a habit of staring at my breasts. He would comment that I was not wearing a bra (in fact I was) and ask if I was trying to seduce him. The first (of the two) took me to a mirror and told me that I looked old and haggard.
>
> One night the same interrogator who used to breathe into my ear, began to blow smoke rings at my nipples.[15] When I got up, trying to get away from him, and threatened to file a complaint, he stopped.[16]

Roni Ben Efrat:

> ...one day the two men who were interrogating me began to laugh at my appearance... They told me that I looked like an "upside-down milk bottle". Then one of them forced me to go and look in the mirror in a bathroom. He accompanied me and stood behind me. This was the first time I had looked in a mirror in the two weeks. He said, "Just see how ugly you look".
>
> There was always one plain-clothes woman soldier on duty in the *Shabak* section. Her job was to escort me to and from my cell and sit in on most of my interrogation sessions. It seemed to be a deliberate policy that all the women assigned to this job should be very conventionally 'attractive'. They were women doing their military service, so they were very young.

Psychological Pressure

Throughout the interrogation period, the underlying goal of the GSS is to find the detainee's weak points. While all the methods of abuse described so far contribute to the building up of psychological as well as physical pressure on the detainee, the GSS also use tactics which are purely psychological.

The aim is to create in the detainee a state of mind in which her determination not to make a confession breaks down. This does not imply that every detainee has something to confess to; there have been a number of cases where the exhausted detainee agreed to sign a false confession drafted for her by the GSS or police (see below, "Case Study"). With female detainees, three types of psychological pressure stand out. Firstly, threats to sexually humiliate the detainee in front of members of her family, and in some cases to rape female relatives. Secondly, detainees who have children describe the manipulation of their maternal feelings, often by lying to them about how their children are faring in their absence. Thirdly, the GSS sometimes try to demoralize the detainee by suggesting that the fact that she, a woman, has been in detention will make her a social outcast in her own society.

Sexual Humiliation

According to Na'ila 'Ayish's lawyer, while the former was in interrogation in February 1987 her interrogators threatened to bring members of her family, including her husband, mother and brothers to the Russian Compound and to rape her in front of them. The interrogators also threatened to Na'ila that they would rape her mother.

For an Arab woman, a threat to sexually humiliate her in front of male relatives is double-edged. It is a threat to hurt and humiliate her, and also, since in traditional Palestinian society men are seen as the guardians of female 'honour', it carries with it the threat of deeply humiliating the men at the same time.

Maryam Qadumi was subjected to a threat to rape her mother and sister:

> One day they said that they would arrest my mother and sister. They said that they would bring them to Jalama, interrogate them and rape them.

As with direct sexual harassment itself, detainees vary in their reactions to this type of threat. Maryam Qadumi:

> At first I took this threat seriously, but later I realized that they did not intend to carry it out.

A Gazan woman interviewed for this report, Ghalia Abu Samra, told of a threat against her husband and boy children. The husband was under interrogation at the same time as Ghalia.

> The *Shabak* told me that they had hit my husband in the testicles, and that he would not be able to give me any more children. They added that they would go to my home and hit my boys in the testicles so that they too would not be able to have children.

There is perhaps a parallel between the message implied in this threat and in the one made to Na'ila 'Ayish: the threat is not only to injure the detainee's loved ones, but also to humiliate them and destroy their power as males.

None of these threats were carried out.

In addition to sexual threats, women detainees are routinely subjected to a wide range of threats against their families and homes. In this respect, they are treated similarly to male detainees.

For example, Iman Jadallah was threatened with having her house burned and her uncle and mother arrested.

Hanan Rahim describes the use of misinformation rather than threats to create in her a state of mind in which she might confess:

> My mother has heart disease. The interrogators knew this and they told me that she had been taken ill and was in hospital. This was a lie.

Manipulation of maternal feelings

Six of the women interviewed about their experiences in interrogation were mothers. Five of these, including the two Jewish Israeli women, said that the GSS deliberately played on their concern for their children. In some cases, this was done by outright lying. In one case, a woman was told that her children would be allowed to visit her, if and only if she confessed.

It is clear that the GSS' intention is to induce in the woman such a state of psychological stress that she agrees to sign a confession. Several of the women said that they felt that their concern about their children was indeed their most vulnerable point.

At the time of her arrest in 1989, Maha Nassar's two children were both under seven. She describes how the GSS tried to play on her concern for them:

> During some of the interrogation sessions I was left alone in the interrogation room. A cassette recorder was playing a tape of children's voices. They were crying, saying things like 'Oh Mama, come back home, we need you!' The tape (which was not of my children) would be played for about 10 minutes. Then the interrogator would come back into the room and say 'Look, we are concerned with your welfare, we want you to go home to your children who need you, we have heard that your children are hungry, nobody is taking care of them, their father is leaving them alone.'

As a very strong woman undergoing her fifth period in detention, Maha was able to analyse the GSS' tactics and resist the intended emotional blackmail. She goes on:

> This was a psychological game. I was feeling very concerned about my children, of course, but all the time I used to think 'if I co-operate in order to be released and get back to my children now, in the future they won't be happy that I got myself released by dishonourable means. My children would be happier to learn that their mother was good and strong and did not talk...'

An even more insidious tactic was used against Salwa Abu Hani.

At the time of Salwa's interrogation in 1987, her daughter was about four. One of the interrogators used to repeat the girl's name constantly during the interrogation sessions. He also wrote her name on pieces of paper. On one occasion he told Salwa that he knew that her daughter was at home, and invited Salwa to telephone her. Salwa refused, suspecting that this was a trick. She thought that the interrogator hoped that if she heard the child's voice, she would break down.

One woman who was breastfeeding her one-year-old son when the GSS arrived to arrest her, said that the worst part of the whole detention experience was being wrenched away from him in the middle of the feed.

> I asked to be allowed to finish feeding him for the last time before being taken away by the *Shabak*. This request was refused, although my son was crying. This was the most inhuman thing they did to me. To ask the *Shabak* to be allowed to feed him for the last time, it was not something dangerous from a security point of view. If I am a 'terrorist', what about my kid? This made me really hate them. It made me want to refuse even to say my name. This was the only thing that made me feel like... I am ready to die... everything is finished, everything is black because I still remember his crying. And he remembers. After they released me, he didn't accept me, he didn't come to say hello to me. For about three days he didn't come and say "Mama"...

Both the Jewish Israeli women report that the GSS told them lies about what was happening to their children in their absence.

Roni Ben Efrat:

> At the time of my interrogation, my two children were aged 12 and 14. I have sole responsibility for them and naturally I was very worried about their welfare without me. The GSS tried to use this to add to the pressure on me. They told me that whoever was asked to care for the children, would be arrested. They also told me that when a parent is arrested, the children are automatically taken to foster parents. They said that I would be sentenced to ten or fifteen years' imprisonment and that when I came out I would be an old woman and my children grown up. On one occasion an interrogator said that he was going to visit the children's school, to speak to their teacher and to my son.

> Sometimes, in the middle of an interrogation session, the interrogator would telephone his home and speak to his children in front of me, acting the 'caring father'. I believe this was a deliberate attempt to make me feel that I was neglecting my children.

In fact, it is not true that the children of detainees are automatically sent to foster parents; and the interrogator did not visit Roni's child's school.

Michal Schwartz:

> The *Shabak* told me that my brother had collected my daughters from the friend who was caring for them. He had taken them against their will and had decided to apply to have legal custody of them. They added that my brother would be sure to give the girls a "Zionist education" and that they would no longer take any notice of me. They would be told that I was a traitor. The *Shabak* also tried to undermine my self-image as a mother, telling me that I had neglected my children and that if I cared about them I would not be in prison now.
>
> I found it hard to believe any of this. [None of it was true.] However, when I appeared doubtful... the interrogators offered to let me telephone my brother and see for myself. I did not accept this offer, because my policy was to accept nothing from them, and I suspected that it was a trick. However, I was left in doubt as to the real whereabouts of the girls.

Comments about social unacceptability of being in detention

Terry Boullata was interrogated at the start of the *intifada*. She says:

> Often during interrogation sessions the *Shabak* would try to taunt me, saying that because I had been in detention nobody would want to marry me. I used to retort that, on the contrary, men would be queuing up to marry me when I got out... One interrogator told me that they could keep me in detention as long as they wanted. I replied that even if they kept me in for 25 years, until I was 46, I would still come out and get married and have children, whereas he would probably be dead by then.

GSS claims to control the legal process

Another form of psychological pressure used by the GSS on all detainees is the making of threats about the way the courts or administrative authorities will deal with the detainee. In making these threats, GSS officers talk as if they, rather than the courts, have control of the legal process.

Michal Schwartz was arrested in April 1988. Three of her colleagues on the newspaper Derech Hanitzotz were already under interrogation. She describes her first interrogation session:

> They said that we were doomed, and that my colleagues and I would receive sentences of fifteen years. They, the GSS, would ensure that

> the evidence against us was indisputable. They also said that, in any event, the court would do what they (the GSS) wanted.[17]

In fact, Michal Schwartz received a sentence of eighteen months.

Maryam Qadumi describes similar threats:

> Another tactic used by the interrogators was to tell me that I would receive a sentence of between ten and twenty years. But the thing that frightened me most, was a threat to have me deported. I did believe this, and I was very worried about it.

Confrontation with potential prosecution witnesses

The GSS sometimes confront the detainee with one or more other detainees who they say have agreed to make statements incriminating the first detainee. This tactic is based on the 'Tamir' amendment in the Israeli law of evidence, whereby a detainee who refuses to confess can be convicted on the written testimony of a third party (see Chapter Three). The clear intent of the GSS is to make the first detainee think that there is no point in refusing to confess. If she does now confess, then of course there will be no need to use statements from the other detainees as the basis of the prosecution against her.

Ghalia Abu Samra's interrogation began on 7 November 1989, in Gaza military centre, at a time when her husband was already under interrogation. She was severely sexually harassed during the first day, but denied the allegations put to her.

> At about 6 o'clock that evening, I was brought face to face with my husband and two youths. The youths said that it was my husband and I who had provided them with guns and money. I thereupon confessed to the matters I was to be charged with.

This GSS tactic is not always so successful, however.

Terry Boullata:

> As time went on and I still refused to make a confession, the *Shabak* appeared to be looking for new ways to pressurize me. One day they confronted me with a young Palestinian who they said had made a statement incriminating me. However, when he saw me he said that I was not the 'Terry' to whom he had been referring in his statement. I laughed. They then beat him in front of me.

Medical Neglect of Sick Detainees

The denial of medical treatment to sick detainees is deliberately used in some cases to add to the pressure on the detainee to confess.

Several of the women interviewed for this report were denied medical treatment which they badly needed during their interrogation. Salwa Abu Hani became ill from lack of food and sleep, which exacerbated her

"Women and children celebrate in Beit Sahour to mark the first anniversary of the declaration of the Palestinian State (on 15 November 1988)." Photographer: *Nadia Sultani*

chronic stomach ulcers (which she says had first developed during an earlier period of imprisonment). Her experience is described in Chapter One under the heading 'Access to Medical Care'.

Salwa Abu Hani did not make a confession and was eventually released without charge. Over three years later, she is still suffering from health problems which are thought to be connected to her maltreatment during this period of interrogation.

The impact of the denial of medical treatment on Na'ila 'Ayish, who began to miscarry early on in her interrogation, is apparent from the legal document quoted below, under the heading "Case Study".

The Jewish Israeli Women: Interrogation Methods Compared

The main difference between the treatment of the Jewish Israeli women interviewed for this report and that of the Palestinian women, is the use of sophisticated psychological techniques and relatively mild sexual harassment with the former, in comparison to physical abuse and more severe sexual harassment with the latter.

The general physical conditions in which the Jewish Israelis were held, may be described as similar to those experienced by the Palestinian women, but less harsh. These have been mentioned in the relevant sections above. Thus the Jewish Israelis were not deprived of food altogether, but the food was barely edible. (Michal Schwartz lost 8–9 kgs during the first ten days and Roni Ben Efrat lost 6 kgs in three weeks.) They were held in dirty, squalid cells without facilities. They were prevented from taking showers for the first few days, but then allowed to shower about every two days. They were not deprived of sleep altogether, but they were regularly interrogated through the night. Unlike the Palestinian detainees, both women saw lawyers during their interrogation period. Roni Ben Efrat was prevented from seeing her lawyer for the first fifteen days, after which she was granted three ten-minute consultations during the second fifteen days. Michal Schwartz first saw her lawyer after seven days (following a High Court challenge to a GSS written order to withhold the visit for fifteen days). She had one or two more brief consultations with the lawyer during the remainder of the interrogation period.

As noted above, the interrogators made it clear from the start of each woman's interrogation that physical pressure would not be used. Michal Schwartz:

> They stressed that they had no intention of using force to make me talk. They said that they would "go by the book", and that their handling of this case would rehabilitate the GSS from the damage done to them by the Landau Commission Report.[18] They talked for hours in this vein.

The sexual harassment to which the Jewish women were subjected has been described above (see 'Sexual Harassment'). They were not threatened with rape nor were they sexually assaulted, although both women describe interrogators sitting uncomfortably close to them and breathing into their ears. One interrogator blew smoke rings at Michal Schwartz's breasts.

Carefully planned psychological pressure was the main strategy used by the GSS to make the Jewish Israeli women talk. In addition to the types of psychological pressure used routinely on all the women, the Jewish women were subjected to pressure in three particular areas.

Firstly, both women were subjected to severe pressure in connection with what the GSS saw as their politics – a process which might be described as "moral blackmail". Roni Ben Efrat:

> On the first night I was interrogated in the middle of the night, by a new interrogator who shouted at me about the Holocaust, saying that I and my friends were 'traitors'.

Michal Schwartz was also called a "traitor". During her first interrogation session, an interrogator tried to put pressure on her by acting out the feelings of anger which (he implied) the average Israeli would have towards her.

> Next, a new interrogator came in. He appeared to be very angry. He began shouting at me that he had been a POW in Syria, and that he had a score to settle with me. He was extremely threatening. He told me that he was not sure whether he could control his feelings of anger.

In addition, both women were told that, now that they were known to be under interrogation for security offences, they would be ostracized by Israeli society and by their families.

Secondly, both women were told that, instead of being subjected personally to physical abuse, Palestinians whom they knew and had worked with as journalists would be brought to the interrogation centre and tortured until they (the women) decided to confess. This threat was carried out. Michal Schwartz:

> I was shown Hani 'Issawi [an ex-colleague and friend] handcuffed in *shabah* on a hot veranda. On one occasion I heard screaming and was told that it was Hani being beaten. I was in the next room. I was also shown a woman who worked in our office, and a man. I was told that these people were being held in Petakh Tikva purely because my colleagues and I refused to confess, and that they would suffer until we did so.

Thirdly the GSS tried to undermine the mental stability of both women. Roni Ben Efrat:

> At one point in my interrogation, I was taken to see a 'psychologist'. I was taken to meet an elderly man, but when I asked who he was, no answer was given. I therefore decided not to speak with him. The interrogator, who was present, began to discuss me with the old man, who made comments as if he was 'analysing' me. He made notes. He told me that I was "unbalanced, nervous and hostile". After he had left, the same interrogator told me that he was going to send me to a mental hospital for fifteen days' observation. He did not in fact do so. However, I found this experience very disturbing.

The use of psychological pressure against Michal Schwartz appears to have been carefully planned. The GSS officers knew a great deal about her personal life, going back to her teenage years. They made this clear in an attempt to unnerve her. She describes her first interrogation session thus:

> ...the first interrogator began by talking to me about the death of my husband and other personal tragedies that had occurred in my past. He seemed to know a great deal about me. He kept telling me that my life had been unhappy and that I appeared not to have learned from my mistakes. This went on for about two hours.

Michal Schwartz made a partial confession after four days, which she then retracted. After this the interrogators intensified the use of psychological pressure, in interrogation sessions that lasted into the early hours of the morning.

> One night, the interrogators told me that they would push me to the point where I would commit suicide... They said that I would receive a sentence of at least eight years' imprisonment. They said that I would be obliged to serve it in solitary confinement, because I would be at risk from Israeli criminal prisoners... and that in the circumstances I would be likely to commit suicide. One of the interrogators said he would be glad if I committed suicide, because I deserved it. He reminded me of the death in detention of Ibrahim al-Rai and said that my case would be the same as his.[19]

In addition to these threats, emphasis was placed on attempts to humiliate Michal Schwartz:

> One night the interrogator who was in the habit of blowing cigarette smoke at me tried a new method of humiliating me. I was offered something to drink and refused. He told me that I was in a state of shock, and on the point of losing my sanity. (I had not spoken to the interrogators for several days.) Then he took a glass of water and a spoon and tried to make me drink from the spoon. I pushed the spoon away and the water splashed over me. This performance was repeated several times.

The use of psychological rather than physical pressure on the Jewish Israeli women is almost certainly a reflection of the GSS' awareness that the former are in a much stronger position to seek redress for physical maltreatment than are Palestinian women. The same applies to psychological maltreatment but, for obvious reasons, the latter is much harder to prove. Despite this, its effectiveness in reducing the detainee to a state of mind in which she or he will confess, should not be underestimated.[20]

Recording the Confession

If a point is reached during the interrogation when the detainee indicates to her interrogators that she is ready to confess, a police officer is called. It is his job to write down the confession. The interrogators usually absent themselves at this point. The police officer writes the confession in Hebrew, which most Palestinian detainees from the Occupied Territories do not understand and certainly cannot read. The detainee will then be asked to sign what the police officer has written.

From the GSS' point of view, there is a major advantage in having a police officer (rather than one of their own officers) record the confession. If the admissibility of the confession is later challenged in court, the police officer can truthfully give evidence that the detainee made the confession to him 'freely and voluntarily', since he will not have been a party to any coercion that may have taken place during the interrogation.

Some of the women interviewed for this report did not make confessions, despite undergoing lengthy interrogations involving various of the techniques described above. Of these women, some were eventually released without charge. At least one was charged on the basis of statements made against her by other detainees.

Others made confessions, were charged, and in due course pleaded guilty to the offences in question, notwithstanding that the confession had been obtained by improper means. Several, however, made confessions which they later sought to retract, on the basis that they were not made 'freely and voluntarily'.

Once a detainee has made a confession, she will be charged and in her subsequent prosecution it will usually be the main if not the sole evidence against her. The legal procedure in which the defendant argues that the confession was not made 'freely and voluntarily' and should therefore not be admitted as part of the evidence, is called the *voir dire* (sometimes also referred to as a 'mini-trial' or 'trial within a trial'). This will be discussed more fully in Chapter Three.

Case Study

The following is the text of a document prepared by the lawyer Felicia Langer for the *voir dire* of Na'ila 'Ayish in August 1987. It is the basis of an argument that Naila's confession should not be heard by the court, because of the means by which it was obtained. The lawyer describes the maltreatment to which Na'ila was subjected, and how this led her to make a confession which was far from 'free and voluntary', and appears to have been false (see paragraphs 31, 34 and 35 (c)).

Arguments prepared for the voir dire *of Na'ila Ibrahim Ayesh, case no. 4084/87, heard August 24 1987 in Ramallah Military Court by a single judge.*

1. The defendant was arrested on 19th February 1987 in Gaza. She was brought to Ashkelon prison and was transferred to prison in Jerusalem on 20 February 1987.

2. She was interrogated by four GSS officers whose names were Abu Nihad, Johnnie, Nisim and another who will be described below. Her interrogation began on 21 February and was characterized by violence, severe physical and mental abuse, degradation of her as a woman and denial of medical treatment. This was in spite of her having informed the interrogators of the fact that she was in the early stages of pregnancy.

3. Her so-called 'confession' is a product of this interrogation. She gave a confession in order to save herself from unbearable abuse and in order to get medical treatment which she badly needed. (The provision of medical treatment was made conditional on her making a confession).

4. At the beginning of the interrogation on 21 February she informed her interrogators that she was in the early stages of pregnancy and that she was bleeding and felt very bad. She said that she was worried about having a miscarriage, and asked to see a doctor. The interrogator's response was that, for the GSS, there was no distinction to be made between her and a man, and that she was considered a terrorist and nothing more.

5. The interrogators used to cover her head with a thick sack which smelled very badly and leave her for hours with her hands tied behind her.

6. *

7. *

8. *

9. The interrogators used the following threats and means of degradation:

(a) a threat to strip her and to rape her in front of another interrogator without a woman prison officer being present (usually one was present);

(b) a threat to bring members of her family including her husband, mother and brothers and to rape her in front of them, and to rape her mother;

(c) curses and insults about her family.

10. Three to four men took part in the interrogation. One used to curse her, another used to hit her and the third played the 'nice guy'. One of the interrogators was particularly cruel. He hit her head on the wall several times. His appearance was as follows: white hair, bulging eyes, glasses, tall and in his thirties. He told her that she was making fun of them and did not want to confess; he compared her to leading figures of organizations, who had carried out operations, and who did not take long to confess.

11. The interrogators took her complaints of severe pain in the belly and womb, bleeding and vomiting, as a pretence. The abuse and the beatings continued. They said they would only stop, and give her medical treatment, if she confessed.

12. On 24 and 25 February, urine samples were taken, supposedly to do a pregnancy test. Na'ila 'Ayish asked for the result and after a long delay was told that she was not pregnant.

13. When the interrogation was resumed, on one occasion she said to the interrogators "you have killed the foetus and you are going to kill me". In response, the interrogator beat her.

14. It is significant that Dr Famush, the prison doctor, subsequently told Dr Muhtadi, Na'ila 'Ayish's doctor, that the urine samples were not tested because they were mixed with blood.

15. It can be seen that the interrogators deliberately lied to the defendant about the results of the test, which in fact was never done.

16. On 5 May 1987, the lawyer Leah Tsemel made a complaint to the Prime Minister's office regarding Na'ila 'Ayish's illegal interrogation and suffering in connection with her pregnancy. In addition, a bail application was filed on 1 March 1987 and was heard by the President of the court. The court ordered that Na'ila 'Ayish should be examined by a doctor. To begin with, the prison authority ignored the decision and she was only examined after repeated requests by Felicia Langer and by Dr. Muhtadi.

17. In a medical report prepared by Dr Muhtadi on 7 May 1987, the defendant was said to have been pregnant and to have miscarried between 22 February and 2 March 1987. The report is based on medical tests, including a pathological test, and the doctor is willing to testify on the defendant's behalf.

18. On 26 February 1987 the defendant made a statement in Arabic denying the offence charged [which was membership of a proscribed organization].

19. Abu Nihad told her that she would receive a sentence of between three and four years because she was contesting the charge and he said "I will write a damning statement about you for the court".

20. The next day the interrogators came to see her and Abu Nihad said to her "you see what you are doing to yourself: you will get

three to four years" and he advised her to retract the denial statement which she had written. She refused.

21. Later on, the interrogators told her "we will forget what you wrote and continue with the interrogation". On the night of 26 to 27 February 1987 the defendant was left outdoors in *shabah*. This was her third night outdoors during the interrogation. It was raining hard and Abu Nihad, who was on night shift, came and lifted the sack from her head and said "you are in luck, it's raining".

22. He began to eat a banana and then offered it to her in a provocative way. He asked her if she was ready to confess.

23. That night the defendant was in a very bad physical and mental condition. She was on the point of breaking. From time to time a policeman came to her and said "we advise you to confess to Abu Nihad because he is the best man we have".

24. At dawn on 27 February Abu Nihad came to her and told her it would be better for her to confess because otherwise the "dogs" would come and then it would be much more difficult for her. (The defendant had not slept all night because she was sitting in *shabah*).

25. On the morning of 27 February, when a policeman came to take her from the yard to the interrogation, when he undid her handcuffs Na'ila fell to the floor. When he realised that she could not stand, he put her on a chair and carried her to the interrogation room. She had no feeling in her legs. Only when she was placed by a heater did the feeling come back. The interrogator said: "you must confess, see what you are doing to yourself".

26. When the interrogators realised that she was still refusing to confess, they left the room and switched on the (cold) air conditioning.

27. By this point Na'ila was in a very bad state and started to vomit. After 5am, four interrogators resumed the interrogation. The one with the bulging eyes started to curse her and ordered the woman prison officer to leave, and also told the other interrogators to leave, saying that he would manage with her by himself. Na'ila told them that what they were doing was illegal. He said to her "So you understand the law, you " and hit her head against the wall.

28. *

29. The interrogator Nisim interfered and said to Na'ila, in a disparaging manner, "you deserved what you got because your strategy is going nowhere".

30. The interrogation session lasted from morning until approximately 10pm, by which time the defendant was feeling utterly weak and desperate. The interrogator Nisim complained that she was forcing him to work until late at night, and that because of her he was unable to see his children who went to sleep at 8pm. He said "Don't you have a heart?"

31. That night, when she was totally weak, she said: "what do you want from me? Do you want me to lie?" Nisim said "Yes, lie". She said "What do you want me to say?" and he replied: "According to our information, you should confess about the letters and about membership in the organization. And if you confess, you will be able to see a doctor, you will be able to take a shower, change your clothes, etc."

32. On 28 February 1987 the interrogation session began in the morning with all the interrogators present, including the man with the bulging eyes and the policeman.

33. The defendant was in a very serious condition, physically weak, mentally broken, depressed because of losing her baby and very frightened about her health both now and in the future. She was in bad need of medical treatment and of a change of clothes. She could not stand the nightmare any longer.

34. She told the interrogator she was ready to admit whatever they wanted. She confessed to membership of the DFLP, and regarding a conversation she had with somebody about studying in Bulgaria. She did this to stop the suffering and to get herself medical treatment.

35. After all this she gave a confession to a policeman in the following circumstances:

(a) the policeman who was sitting with her had a piece of paper in front of him and he asked her questions from the paper. When her answers did not coincide with what was written on the paper, he said to her "you didn't say that to the GSS, and everything should conform to what is written here on this piece of paper."

(b) Abu Nihad came in and out.

(c) After the "confession" was taken, she was asked to sign and she said "how can I sign something which is a lie?"

(d) The policeman stopped and called Abu Nihad, who said to the defendant "OK, if you don't sign we'll start everything all over again from the beginning.

From the above, it is clear that the confession was not made voluntarily, and therefore it should not be admitted in evidence by the court.

Felicia Langer, Advocate [21]

* Paragraphs 6,7, 8 and 28 are illegible in the original and have therefore been omitted.

Notes

1. Military Order 29 "Order Concerning the Running of Prison Institutions".
2. She is unlikely to have been told of precise charges.

3. As opposed, for example, to being held for a few hours and then released, or charged with a very minor offence without interrogation, or held as a hostage pending the arrest of another member of her family.
4. Between 1987 and 1990, eight Palestinian men died under interrogation. (Figures supplied by al-Haq.)
5. Na'ila Ayesh says that she told the interrogators about her pregnancy immediately. The response was "You are like a man and there is no difference about that and it does not matter to us." She miscarried during the interrogation.
6. In the interviews, the women often referred to the GSS as the *Shabak*. This word has not been changed to "GSS", in order to reflect more accurately the way the interviewee spoke.
7. See *Israel's Use of Electric Shock Torture in the Interrogation of Palestinian Detainees*, published by Palestine Human Rights Information Centre in December 1991 and an article entitled *Torture Unit* by Doron Mei'iri in *Hadashot* newspaper, 24 February 1992.
8. Accounts of interrogation methods given to human rights organizations by women ex-detainees are so markedly similar to each other that there can be little room for doubt as to their accuracy. In February 1990 the Jerusalem branch of the Israeli group the Women's Organization for Political Prisoners published an account of the methods used, together with a set of testimonials by ex-detainees. In the ensuing public furore, MK Shevakh Weiss, *Ma'arakh* member of the Knesset Committee on Foreign Affairs and Security, was invited to visit the *Shabak* section of the Russian Compound (presumably in the hope he would conclude that the WOFPP's information was inaccurate and exaggerated. He did come to this conclusion, in the TV interview he gave after the visit, but he also confirmed the use of *shabah*, and of the 'coffin' and of the *zinzana* or tiny isolation cell. He did not see anything wrong in these methods. Weiss concluded: "It is not pleasant. I don't envy anyone who has to go through this experience. Nevertheless, I didn't get the impression that it is similar to... Solzhenitsyn's description of the "gulags" ... a difficult place, but not threatening." (from the Israeli newspaper "*Yerushelayim*", 3 March 1990.)
9. These included threats to rape Jadallah and to arrest her mother and uncle and to burn her house.
10. The lawyer attested to having seen this rash when she visited Jadallah on August 6 1990.
11. MO 29 Order Concerning the Running of Prison Institutions
12. The Palestinian Israelis interviewed for this report did not describe as severe sexual harassment as did some of the Palestinians from the Occupied Territories. However, the number of Palestinian Israelis interviewed was too small for one to make a reliable generalization that this is the norm.
13. An English translation of the affidavit was published in *April 17th* newsletter. The blanks appear in the English translation.

14. During the *intifada*, there have been reports of women being kidnapped, coerced into undressing and then being photographed with men, in an attempt to blackmail them into becoming 'collaborators'. Little has been written about this.
15. Michal Schwartz was fully clothed.
16. Later on, during the trial, a senior police officer admitted under cross examination that this interrogator had told him about the incident and that they had laughed about it together. This appears in the transcript of the trial.
17. In addition to this, the GSS gave Michal crucially wrong information about her legal right to remain silent.
18. See Chapter Four under the heading "The Landau Commission Report". Roni Ben Efrat and Michal Schwartz were both arrested in April 1988, some seven months after the report's publication.
19. Ibrahim al-Rai died in detention shortly before the arrest of the *Derech Hanitzotz* journalists, in circumstances that were not at all clear. The official explanation for his death was "suicide".
20. In fact it was the sending of forged notes purporting to be from one of their colleagues, in which he supposedly urged them to confess, which eventually persuaded both the women quoted above to make confessions.
21. This case is discussed further in Appendix Four.

Chapter Three
The Trial

The Right to a 'fair and regular trial'

Having established that confessions are very often obtained from women detainees by the use of physical and psychological abuse, often amounting to 'torture', we now consider how this affects the right of a suspect to a 'fair and regular trial'. In international humanitarian law this right is of crucial importance. It is guaranteed to people facing trial in occupied territories, during international as well as internal armed conflicts. Article 3 common to all four Geneva Conventions of 1949,[1] which applies to "conflicts not of an international character", prohibits:

> [T]he passing of sentences and the carrying out of executions without previous judgment pronounced by a regularly constituted court, affording all the judicial guarantees which are recognized as indispensable by civilized peoples.

As Dr. Jean Pictet makes clear in his authoritative Commentary to Article 3 of the Fourth Geneva Convention of 1949:

> All civilized nations surround the administration of justice with safeguards aimed at eliminating the possibility of judicial errors. The Convention has rightly proclaimed that it is essential to do so in time of war.[2]

Therefore, it is not surprising that Article 147 of the Convention makes the wilful deprivation of a fair and regular trial a 'grave breach' of the convention. (*All* states party to the Convention have a *legal duty* to "seek out and prosecute" or extradite elsewhere for trial any person involved in committing a grave breach.)

So far as the Occupied Territories are concerned, as "protected persons" under Article 4 of the Fourth Geneva Convention, Palestinian women in the West Bank and Gaza Strip have some specific safeguards guaranteed to them, in particular under Articles 71 and 72 of the Convention. The first paragraph of Article 71 provides the general rule:

> No sentence shall be pronounced by the competent courts of the Occupying Power except after a regular trial.

The concept of a 'regular trial' involves several elements, and is not confined to what happens in the court room itself. It encompasses the protection of the defendant's rights from the time of arrest to the conclusion of the trial. This means that there are a long list of 'due process' rights which must all be present for a detainee to have a 'fair and regular' trial. The reader is referred to Appendix II for the full list of rights and an explanation of how Israel is legally bound to ensure that Palestinians in the Occupied Territories benefit from them. For now, it is important to focus on the following:

1. The right
(a) not to be subjected to physical or moral coercion, in particular in order to obtain information from the detainee or from 'third parties'; and not to be subjected to any measure of such a character as to cause her physical suffering, including torture and any other measures of brutality whether applied by "civilian or military agents"; and
(b) the concomitant right not to be compelled to testify against herself or to confess guilt.
2. The right to be presumed innocent until she is proved guilty.
3. The right to "all necessary rights and means of defence". More particularly:
(a) The right to present evidence necessary to her defence and call witnesses; and
(b) The right to be assisted by a qualified advocate or counsel of her own choice, who is able to visit her freely and enjoy the necessary facilities for preparing the defence.
4. The right to be aided by an interpreter, *both during the preliminary investigation and during the hearing in court* and the right "*at any time* to object to the interpreter and to ask for his replacement".[3]

The Denial of a 'fair and regular trial' in the Occupied Territories

As can be seen from the rights listed above, it is clearly envisaged that a detainee should have an effective means of preventing her 'confession' being heard by a trial court, where it was obtained by physical or moral coercion, torture or any other measures of brutality. However, Palestinian women facing trial before military courts in the Occupied Territories face an almost impossible task in this respect.

Trying to exclude confession evidence

In most legal systems, not all relevant evidence is 'admissible' evidence at the trial of someone charged with a criminal offence. The term 'admissible' is lawyers' shorthand for the rules which govern what evidence can be heard by a court. Therefore, challenging the admissibility of a confession involves the defendant or her lawyer arguing at a preliminary hearing that the confession should not be used (or 'admitted') as part of the evidence against her, because it was obtained in breach of the rules of evidence. If the challenge is upheld by the court, then the confession is not supposed to be taken into account by the court at all when it hears all the admissible evidence during the trial itself. (If the prosecution has little or no evidence besides the confession, as is common in security trials in the military courts, then the prosecution case will collapse at this stage.)

As a 1964 UN study of the legal systems of over ninety countries found, many countries "limit or prohibit the use of confessions or incriminating statements as evidence against the accused, if there is ground to believe that such statements have been made under improper conditions."[4] These limitations are not necessarily based on the presumption that the truth of such statements cannot be trusted; the main purpose is "rather to provide an effective deterrent against the use of improper methods of interrogation."[5] Nevertheless, such limitations are clearly designed to ensure that the defendant receives a 'fair and regular trial': courts are supposed to decide whether defendants are innocent or guilty only on the basis of facts which have been proven by reliable and fairly obtained evidence.

In the Israeli criminal courts, the basic rule concerning the confession evidence is that it is admissible "only when the prosecution has produced evidence as to the circumstances in which it was made and the court is satisfied that it was free and voluntary".[6] Therefore, an 'evidential burden of proof' is formally placed on the prosecution to show that a confession was made voluntarily. In the military courts in the West Bank and Gaza, a similar rule applies. Section 477 of the Military Justice Law, 1955, states that:

> A military court shall not admit the confession of an accused as evidence unless it is convinced that the accused made it of his own free will.

The difference between the civilian rule of evidence and the military one is significant if subtle: in the latter case the prosecution is not formally required to prove voluntariness. Instead, a military court just has to be "convinced" the confession was made voluntarily.[7]

The voir dire *procedure*

When the defence wish to challenge the admissibility of an alleged confession, the court holds what is called a *voir dire* or 'trial within a trial'. The *voir dire* procedure used in the military courts is similar to that used in ordinary criminal courts in Israel. It works as follows.

At a remand hearing prior to the trial, the defence lawyer applies for leave to hold a *voir dire*. This is usually granted. The lawyer then indicates to the court which prosecution witnesses are required for cross examination (ie GSS and police officers), and a date is set. However, the unavailability of GSS officers often causes *voir dire* hearings to be adjourned, leading to long delays.[8]

When the *voir dire* hearing does finally take place, the prosecution calls its witnesses as to the circumstances in which the confession was obtained, and the defence cross examine them about this. For example, the GSS officers who interrogated the defendant may give evidence that the defendant offered to confess voluntarily; then the defence may cross examine them to the effect that the 'confession' was only made following the use of violence or threats towards the defendant. The defendant may also give evidence as to the treatment which preceded her making the alleged confession. The court will then have to decide whether it accepts the prosecution or defence version and, on the basis of that, whether the confession was made voluntarily. If not, then it cannot be heard at trial. Alternatively, if the court is "convinced" the confession was made voluntarily, then when the trial begins the actual confession statement will be heard by the court. It should be added that, as in many other countries, no Israeli court can convict a defendant on the basis of a confession alone: there must be some supporting evidence of guilt.[9] This is called the *dvar ma* or *scintilla*. However, it can be something altogether trivial, for example the actual existence of a person, place or event referred to in the confession.[10]

Proving Abuse

It is extremely difficult for an individual to establish in a court of law, whether during a *voir dire* or in a civil action for assault, that she was tortured by the GSS. First, the interrogators are very careful to avoid using methods which will leave lasting visible marks. If a woman receives bruises, she will usually be held incommunicado until they have disappeared.[11] Injuries resulting from prolonged periods of *shabah* are likely to be muscular or skeletal, and without visible manifestations. In the rare cases where hospital treatment is administered to a detainee during the interrogation period (more common among men), the medical records sometimes disappear or are not made in the correct name, and so cannot be connected to her.[12] Psychological damage, for example resulting from threats of rape and sexual harassment, is extremely hard to prove. To some extent the GSS can rely on women's reluctance to talk about it publicly as a guarantee against redress.

Another factor which makes it difficult to prove abuse is the anonymity of GSS officers. In the presence of detainees they refer to each other by Arab pseudonyms, (eg "Abu Sharif").[13] They wear civilian clothes without marks of identification; and they are not seen in public places frequented by those they interrogate. Thus, even if a woman were able to prove that she had suffered specific harm during interrogation, it would be very difficult for her to establish by whom.

Last, there is the very obvious problem that the detainee is alone without witnesses who would be prepared to speak on her behalf. In an Israeli military court; the evidence of one or more GSS officers will invariably be preferred to hers. Even if the court accepts that some abuse has been proven, as we shall see in Chapter Four a certain amount of abuse is officially permitted and confessions obtained in this way are therefore regularly admitted in evidence. In the light of all of the above it is not surprising that, in practice, it is almost unheard of for the defence to win a *voir dire* in a military court; or that, according to the Israeli human rights organization B'tselem, a *voir dire* will fail "even in the rare cases where the defence produces external evidence (such as a medical report)".[14]

Inevitable conviction following an unsuccessful voir dire

In effect, after the *voir dire* has been lost, the whole trial is lost: when the confession is heard by the court, the conviction of the defendant becomes inevitable.

Once the confession is admitted into evidence a great deal of weight is placed on it. As with Diplock (non-jury) Courts which hear 'terrorist offences' in Northern Ireland, after an Israeli military court has admitted a confession into evidence it does not make a "subsequent inquiry specifically to deal with the reliability of the confession."[15] In other words, the court having found the 'confession' to have been made 'voluntarily', it makes no further enquiry as to the reliability or even the truth of its contents. Thus, prosecution-minded judges make findings of fact based almost exclusively on contested confessions, ignoring their possible unreliability.

Discouraging voir dires

Since it is so very rare for the defence to win a *voir dire*, defendants and their lawyers rarely ask for them. This means that, in practice, contested trials of security offences are rare. (For, when the basis of the prosecution case is the confession, if the defendant does not challenge its admissibility then he or she cannot contest the charges, given the court's inevitable and unrebuttable assumption that the confession is reliable.)

In addition to the near impossibility of being successful, there are two other disincentives to defendants to challenge their 'confessions'. First, as was pointed out earlier, holding a *voir dire* invariably causes long delays in the hearing of the case. Second, it has been noted that those convicted after an unsuccessful *voir dire* receive heavier sentences. B'tselem reports that "all defence lawyers agree that this happens."[16]

The likely outcome, then, for the defendant who holds a *voir dire* is that she will nevertheless be convicted, and will receive a longer sentence than she would otherwise have had. For all of these reasons, and because they have no faith in the military court system, the vast majority of defendants on security charges take the pragmatic option of a plea bargain. This means that the defence lawyer negotiates with the prosecutor as to which charges the defendant will admit and what length of sentence the judge will be asked to pass on him or her, and whatever is agreed is presented to the court for 'rubber-stamping'.

It is also quite common, in situations where the defence have decided to hold a *voir dire*, for a plea bargain to be agreed at the last moment, with the result that the *voir dire* does not go ahead. An example of this is the case of Fatma Abu Bakra (see Chapter Two). Fatma made a confession as the result of severe sexual harassment, and decided to challenge its admissibility. Shortly before the trial, the prosecution proposed to the defence lawyer, Leah Tsemel, that they would ask for a relatively low sentence, if the defence would agree not to hold the *voir dire*. The sentence to be asked for was five years. This was proposed at the instigation of the GSS, who did not want Fatma's claim to have been sexually harassed by her interrogators to be put before a court.

As Fatma and her lawyer realised that they were extremely unlikely to be successful in the *voir dire*, and since the sentence proposed by the prosecution was lower than the sentence she would get if she fought the *voir dire* and lost, they decided to accept the prosecution's proposal. Usually, judges in the military courts abide by deals on sentences agreed by the prosecution and defence in advance of the trial. In this case, the judge sentenced Fatma to two years more than had been agreed, so she lost out both ways: she did not get any satisfaction in exposing the GSS methods and she did not get the shorter sentence.[17] On appeal, her sentence was reduced from seven to six years.

The abuse experienced by Na'ila 'Ayish during interrogation in February 1987, before the *intifada*, has been referred to in Chapter Two. She told her lawyer that her confession had been made under severe duress, and a decision was made to challenge its admissibility at the trial. Her lawyer, Felicia Langer, prepared a written statement – quoted in full in the Case Study at the end of Chapter Two – for the application for leave to hold a *voir dire*. The *voir dire* was never in fact held. The prosecution offered a plea bargain under which Na'ila would receive a suspended sentence, and this was accepted by the defence. The GSS tried to make it a condition of the 'deal' that Na'ila would withdraw her allegations against them, but she did not do so.

Other rules of evidence designed to secure convictions

Amnesty International has reported that "most sources agree that confessions are the primary evidence in the great majority of cases".[18] Nevertheless, occasionally a confession is not obtained from the detainee or appears to need strengthening by additional evidence. Even less often, a *voir dire* is successful. However, even in such cases certain rules of evidence can still produce a miscarriage of justice. For instance, in principle Rule 9 of Military Order 378 requires the military courts to follow the same rules of evidence as apply in the Israeli criminal courts. However, the same Rule provides that "...a military court is entitled to deviate from the rules of evidence for special reasons that shall be stated, if it considers it is necessary to do so."[19] Even more alarming is the use that can be made of 'confessions' made by third parties, following the 'Tamir Amendment' to the rules of evidence.

The 'Tamir Amendment'

This amendment of the Israeli law of evidence in criminal trials provides that defendants who refuse to sign a confession can be prosecuted and convicted on the basis of a written statement by a third party without the evidence being given live in court.[20] In most common law criminal justice systems, a statement made by someone other than the defendant can only be used as part of the prosecution case if this person (the third party) comes to court and repeats it in the witness stand. Thus a statement made to police which the maker is unwilling to repeat in court (for whatever reason) cannot form part of the prosecution case. This rule is part of the rule against 'hearsay' and is designed to protect the defendant against the use of fabricated or unreliable evidence. The principle is that all testimony on which the defendant stands to be convicted should be given live in court, and the defendant or her lawyer should be given the opportunity to test it by cross-examination of the witness, in order to demonstrate prejudice, hostility or unreliability.[21] It is arguable that any denial of this right is a breach of the defendant's right to "all necessary rights and means of defence", mentioned above, and that invoking the Tamir Amendment in any case involves a denial of a suspect's right to a fair and regular trial.[22]

The Tamir Amendment was passed in 1980.[23] Different lawyers give different accounts as to why it was introduced. Some say the background was judicial concern about the making of threats against prosecution witnesses in large-scale 'underworld' criminal trials, with the result that the witnesses refused to testify and the defendants had to be acquitted. Others say it was the case of the extradition from the US of Ziyad Abu 'Ain, a Palestinian whom the Israelis wanted to try on charges relating to a military operation. The US courts agreed to the extradition, making it a condition that he be tried in the Israeli criminal courts and that the proceedings be fair. The problem for the Israelis was that Ziyad Abu 'Ain had not made a confession, and the only evidence which the prosecution had was in the form of written statements by third parties who were not available to testify. The law was amended so as to allow the defendant to be prosecuted on the basis of the written statements, and he was convicted.

The Amendment continues to apply in the Israeli criminal courts, and is widely used there in non-security trials. In the military courts, it is also used frequently. Often, when a detainee refuses to confess under interrogation, the GSS will try to obtain a statement incriminating him or her from another detainee. They may use similar methods to obtain this statement to those they use to get confessions. If they are successful, and the third party signs the incriminating statement, which may be written in Hebrew, it can be used as the basis of a prosecution of the detainee who did not confess. If there is a trial and the third party either fails to attend or attends but refuses to repeat what is in the statement, then the written version will be produced. The judge then has to decide whether to accept the statement in evidence or to exclude it due to the witness' non-attendance, silence or his claims that he made the statement as a result of torture. Practising lawyers report that, in security cases, the judge invariably decides to accept the written statement. As mentioned earlier, some supporting evidence is required for the defendant to be convicted, but it can be something of relatively little weight, and easy to obtain, such as an unsigned confession.[24] Such evidence is easy to fabricate and its authenticity is difficult to challenge. The GSS can simply get a police officer to draft a confession, and when he gives evidence he will say that the detainee gave him the confession but refused to sign it.[25]

It is not known how widely the Tamir Amendment is relied on in prosecutions for security offences. Lawyers who defend in security cases hold varying views on this. Some say it is widely used; others say that the threat of its use is relied on by the GSS as an additional pressure to persuade the detainee to confess. Certainly, from the detainee's point of view, there is little point in trying to remain silent through days or weeks of maltreatment and torture if the end result is likely to be that you are convicted on the basis of a written statement by a third party. Also, defendants who are prosecuted on the basis of third party statements face the same disincentives to having a contested trial as those prosecuted on the basis of a confession: they know that the court will be highly unlikely to accept their challenges to the evidence, and that the months spent waiting for trial will increase the overall time they spend in prison.

Limiting the right to silence

Finally, the right to silence is severely restricted in trials held before Israeli military courts. The right to silence is a fundamental one, which derives from the connected principles that the defendant must be presumed innocent until proven guilty (see the second-numbered right to a 'fair and regular trial' set out earlier) and that it is for the prosecution to prove the defendant's guilt, not for the defendant to prove his or her innocence. In the military courts, the defendant's silence during interrogation cannot be used against her. Her refusal to give evidence at her trial, however, may be so used, as may her failure to deny the charge when it is put to her at an extension of detention hearing. The latter rule is particularly harsh, given the subsequent use which an interrogator might make of a detainee's silence at such a hearing. The defendant's failure to answer either "guilty" or "not guilty" when the charge is read out at the start of the trial, may also be used in support of the prosecution case. These rules constitute a serious additional breach of a defendant's right to a 'fair and regular' trial.

Notes

1. See Appendix I for a summary of the provisions of the Fourth Geneva Convention of 1949 and an explanation of the distinction between humanitarian law and human rights law. Appendix I also explains why the Fourth Geneva Convention of 1949 applies to Israel's occupation of the

West Bank and Gaza Strip. See Appendix II for a detailed discussion of the right to a fair trial under international law.

2. Jean Pictet (ed.), *Commentary on the Fourth Geneva Convention Relative to the Protection of Civilian Persons in Time of War*, 1958, (Pictet) 39.
3. See Appendix II for full references to where each of these rights is to be found.
4. United Nations Department of Economic and Social Affairs, *Study of the right of everyone to be free from arbitrary arrest, detention and exile* (UN Study), 1964, (E/CN.4/826/Rev.1), para 416.
5. Ibid.
6. Evidence Ordinance, 1971, section 12(2).
7. A similar effect has been achieved in Northern Ireland, under section 8 of the Emergency Provisions Act, 1991. See the Haldane Society of Socialist Lawyers, *Upholding the rule of law ? Northern Ireland: criminal justice under the "emergency powers" in the 1990s*, 1992, 36.
8. See B'tselem, *The Interrogation of Palestinians During the Intifada: ill-treatment, "moderate physical pressure" or torture?*, March 1991, (B'tselem Report), 101102, where the case of Yusuf Inkawi is cited. His *voir dire* was apparently postponed more than twenty times, "as the witnesses did not appear."
9. See UN Study, para 430.
10. See Report of an International Commission of Jurists (ICJ) Mission by Jordan J Paust, Gerhard von Glahn and Guenter Woratsch, *Inquiry into the Israeli military court system in the West Bank and Gaza*, 1990, (ICJ Report), 33; and Amnesty International, *The military justice system in the Occupied Territories: detention, interrogation and trial procedures*, July 1991, AI index: MDE 15/34/91 (AI Report), 69
11. This is one of several ways in which torture is officially concealed. See al-Haq, *A nation under siege*, 1990, 169171.
12. See ibid, 170–171 for two examples of "unrecorded" visits to hospital by detainees.
13. The use of Arab pseudonyms by Israeli interrogators was highlighted by Palestine Human Rights Information Centre in *Israel's Use of Electric Shock Torture in the Interrogation of Palestinian Detainees*, published in December 1991 and by Doron Mei'iri in an article entitled "Torture Unit", published by *Hadashot* on 24 February 1992. Also, Arab pseudonyms were favoured by Israeli interrogators involved in torturing five of the seven individuals whose cases are set out in detail in the B'tselem Report, 75–96.
14. See the B'tselem Report, quoted above, 101: "successes in mini-trials [*voir dires*] are few." Also, see AI Report, 67.
15. Douwe Korff, *The Diplock Courts in Northern Ireland: A fair trial?* , April 1984, SIM Special No 3, 66. See also Steven Greer and Anthony White, *Abolishing the Diplock Courts*, 1986, 17.
16. B'tselem Report, 101.

17. In addition, Fatma had to deal with a very negative response from her community in Gaza, who took the view that since she did not go ahead with the *voir dire*, her allegations against the interrogators must have been false. (Fatma was released from custody on 26 November 1991, one year before the end of her sentence. See Palestine Human Rights Information Centre, *Human Rights Update*, Vol 4, No 11, November 1991, 270.)
18. AI Report, 49 see footnote 10; and ICJ Report, 32.
19. It is interesting to note that the precedent for allowing the military court to deviate from the rules of evidence is in the British Defence (Emergency) Regulations of 1945; then however, the court was required only to do so "in the interests of justice". There is no such safeguard in the present Israeli Military Order.
20. Law of Evidence, section 10(a). Cf section 23 of the British Criminal Justice Act 1988, but note section 26 thereof.
21. See, The European Court of Human Rights, *Bricmont* -v- *Belgium*, Series A, No. 158, para. 81. and *Kostovski* -v- *Netherlands*, Series A, No 166, paras 4243.
22. For the contrary view, see Stephanos Stavros, "The right to a fair trial in Emergency Situations", *International and Comparative Law Quarterly*, Vol. 41, 1992, 343, at 356357. Cf ICJ, States of emergency, 1983, 430 & 462; and Oraa, *Human rights in states of emergency in international law*, 1992, 113"114. According to the ICJ, one of the ways in which the ill-treatment of detainees (who will eventually face criminal charges) is facilitated is by changes in the law of evidence. This is because these changes encourage greater reliance on confession and limit the defendant's right to contest evidence collected during the investigatory stage.
23. Tamir was then Justice Minister.
24. AI Report, 69.
25. Supreme Court decisions since 1980 have loosened the rules concerning the type of third party statement which can be used under the Amendment, so that the statement does not have to be signed by its maker and it does not have to have been contemporaneously recorded.

Chapter Four
Does Israel Sanction Torture?

In this Chapter, Israel's international obligation not to torture will be explained and set with official Israeli policy and the lack of any effective measures to prevent the GSS from torturing or ill-treating Palestinian women security detainees.

Torture Defined

To determine whether Palestinian women have been 'tortured', rather than simply ill-treated, by the GSS, the treatment described in Chapter Two should be compared with the definition of torture contained in the UN Convention Against Torture and Other Cruel, Inhuman or Degrading Treatment or Punishment of 1984 (UN Convention Against Torture). Article 1 of that Convention defines torture as:

> [A]ny act by which severe pain or suffering, whether physical or mental, is intentionally inflicted on a person for such purposes as obtaining from him or a third person information or a confession, punishing him for an act he or a third person has committed or is suspected of having committed, or intimidating or coercing him or a third person, or for any reason based on discrimination of any kind, when such pain or suffering is inflicted by or at the instigation of or with the consent or acquiescence of a public official or other person acting in an official capacity. It does not include pain or suffering arising only from, inherent in or incidental to lawful sanctions.

Nearly all of the forms of pressure described in Chapter Two amount to 'torture' within the above definition: most of the women interviewed suffered "severe pain or suffering", either physical or mental or both; the "motive" in each case was one or more of the specified "purposes"; and the perpetrators were public officials or other persons "acting in an official capacity."

Israel's international obligations not to torture

Israel is bound by three international conventions which contain prohibitions against the use of torture. The Fourth Geneva Convention Relative to the Protection of Civilian Persons in Time of War, of 12 August 1949, was ratified by Israel on 10 April 1951. Israel is almost alone among world legal opinion in refusing to accept that this Convention applies to its occupation of the West Bank and Gaza Strip. However, Israel claims to abide voluntarily by what it calls the "humanitarian provisions" of the Convention.[1] The following provisions of the Convention are relevant:

Article 31

> No physical or moral coercion shall be exercized against protected persons, in particular to obtain information from them or third parties.

Article 32

> The High Contracting Parties specifically agree that each of them is prohibited from taking any measure of such a character as to cause the physical suffering or extermination of protected persons in their hands. This prohibition applies not only to murder, torture, corporal punishments, mutilation and medical or scientific experiments..., but also to any other measures of brutality whether applied by civilian or military agents.

[In the case of the Israeli occupation virtually all the inhabitants of the West Bank and Gaza Strip are "protected persons", as defined under Article 4 of the Convention.]

In 1984 the UN Convention Against Torture was entered into. The treaty came into force in 1987, when a sufficient number of states had ratified it. Israel signed the UN Convention Against Torture on 22 October 1986. Once a state has signed a treaty, it is constrained from taking any action which is inconsistent with the main purposes of that treaty pending its ratification.[2] In the case of this treaty, Israel was at least bound to prevent people under its jurisdiction from being tortured. Israel ratified the UN Convention Against Torture on 3 October 1991. (This was about one year after the interviews on which this report is based had been conducted.) The definition of 'torture' in Article 1 of that Convention is set out above. Article 2 provides:

> 1. Each State Party shall take effective legislative, administrative, judicial or other measures to prevent acts of torture in any territory under its jurisdiction.
>
> 2. No exceptional circumstances whatsoever, whether a state of war or threat of war, internal political instability or any other public emergency, may be invoked as a justification of torture.
>
> 3. An order from a superior officer or a public authority may not be invoked as a justification for torture.

On the same day that it ratified the UN Convention Against Torture, Israel also ratified the International Covenant of Civil and Political Rights of 1966 (ICCPR). Article 7 of the Covenant provides that:

> None shall be subjected to torture or to cruel, inhuman or degrading treatment or punishment...

As well as international treaties forbidding torture, Israel is legally bound by the absolute prohibition of torture under customary international law, which the UN Convention Against Torture reflects.[3]

Israel is therefore under a clear duty not to torture. The testimonies quoted in Chapter Two show that Israel is in breach of this duty. Indeed, the situation appears to be even more serious than this: there is evidence that the Israeli authorities expressly authorize acts which constitute torture and that officials giving out this treatment are acting in accordance with instructions. The most important evidence of this is the Report of the 'Landau Commission' of 30 October 1987 and the way its recommendations have been implemented.

The Landau Commission Report

On 31 May 1987 the Israeli Government decided to establish a "Commission of Inquiry into the Investigation Methods of the General Security Services Regarding Hostile Terrorist Activity". The Commission's brief was to examine the "methods and procedures" of the GSS and "the giving of testimony in court in connection with these investigations".[4] The Commission was headed by a retired High Court Judge, Moshe Landau. The other two members were generals from the military reserves. It seems that Advocate Terlo, a legal representative of the GSS, attended all the deliberations of the Commission, which "took evidence from GSS officers, read reports on security work during the previous twenty years, analysed the law relevant to methods of interrogation and wrote a report with recommendations."

Background to the Landau Commission

The background to the decision to set up the Commission was public concern about the practices of the GSS following the 'No.300 Bus Affair' and 'the Nafsu case'. Izzat Nafsu was a Circassian officer in the Israeli army who was arrested in 1980 and charged with offences against the state. He was convicted on the basis of a confession and sentenced to eighteen years in prison. At his trial, Nafsu had challenged the admissibility of his confession in evidence, saying that it was made as a result of physical and psychological coercion. However, the prosecution denied his allegations and the defence evidence was rejected by the court.

Then came the 'Bus 300 revelations', which showed that senior GSS officials had obstructed an inquiry into the security forces' summary execution of two Palestinians who had hijacked an Israeli bus in Gaza. As a consequence of these revelations, Nafsu was able to identify a senior GSS agent as the commander of the team of his interrogators. The new head of the GSS therefore ordered an internal inquiry into his case. In the course of this inquiry, those who had interrogated Nafsu (having received

"Women gathering outside the house of a martyr, minutes after the killing (by the army), in a village near Hebron."

Photographer: *Nadia Sultani*

a promise of a pardon in advance) admitted that most of his allegations were true. Even more significant was the claim by Nafsu's interrogators that "in using means of pressure they had not gone beyond what was allowed to them in the GSS directives that existed at the time". (para 2.5)[5]

Findings and Recommendations of the Landau Commission

Although the Commission's Report was 'published' in October 1987, an Appendix was kept secret and has never been made public. The basic conclusion of the Commission was that the use of psychological and "moderate physical" pressure during interrogations of those suspected of "hostile terrorist activity" ("HTA") was not only necessary, but permissible under the law as it stood. Lying by GSS officers when giving evidence about their interrogation methods was, however, utterly unacceptable, and must stop.

The Report makes clear that it uses the term "hostile terrorist activity" to refer to the activities of all nationalist-minded Palestinians, regardless of their politics or those of the political group which they support. It refers to all of the Palestinian political groups as the "Arab terror organizations" and declares that "the objective of the terrorist organizations is the destruction of the State of Israel..." (para 2.9) This is not correct, of course, in relation to several Palestinian political groups.

The Report goes on to describe the difficulties encountered by the GSS in interrogating those suspected of "hostile terrorist activity", supposedly due to their determination not to reveal information:

> [T]he interrogation of an HTA suspect by the GSS turns into a difficult confrontation between the vital need to discover what he knows... and the will of the person interrogated to keep silent and conceal what he knows or to mislead the interrogators by providing false information. (para 2.18)

It is acknowledged that in most trials of those allegedly involved in "hostile terrorist activity", the sole evidence is the confession. The Commission states that its secret Appendix to the Report includes a survey of interrogation methods used by the GSS from 1967 onwards, "and of the permission given to interrogators from time to time to employ means of pressure, including physical pressure." It adds that among GSS interrogators, the prevailing view is that "recourse to some measure of physical pressure... is unavoidable." (para 2.21) In examining why GSS officers lied in court about the use of physical pressure, the Report cites three reasons given to them by the interrogators who testified before the Commission. First, the need to keep their methods secret; second, the need to ensure that convictions were obtained; third, the ease with which the interrogators obtained the trust of judges. The reader gets the impression that the concept of the due process of law is not regarded with great respect by the GSS. Indeed, many of the GSS officers who testified before the Commission gave the following type of rationalization for lying:

"Interrogation work for uncovering HTA is a sacred mission which justifies the means, any means" and "security is above the law". (para 2.40) They insisted, however, that strenuous efforts are made to ensure that the content of a confession is true, before it is used in evidence. This is unconvincing. Where a confession is the sole evidence available, it is not clear how its veracity can be checked. Meanwhile, cases are known where people have made false confessions purely to avoid being tortured.[6]

This part of the Report ends with a strong condemnation of the GSS, *not* for using physical abuse and torture, but for committing perjury in court when testifying about their methods.[7] Amazingly, the Report goes on to "note with satisfaction that this harmful practice [of perjury] has now been totally abolished" (para 2.33). One wonders on what this is based, given the contradictions in the Report. On the one hand the Commission asserts that GSS officers will now tell the truth about their methods when called to give evidence in court. On the other hand the Commission insists on the need for secrecy about GSS interrogation methods: both the description of methods used in the past and guidelines for the future are consigned to the *secret* Appendix. To say that GSS officers now always tell the truth is, therefore, both misleading and disingenuous.

The next part of the Report deals with "legal and moral" aspects of the question of interrogation methods. It acknowledges that there are provisions in Israeli criminal and civil law which might be breached when an interrogator uses physical pressure on a detainee. However, the Report continues, Israeli criminal law has a defence of 'necessity'. It is claimed that an interrogator charged with, for example, the criminal offence of assault, could raise 'necessity' in his defence. The necessity defence appears in section 22 of the Penal Law of 1977:

> A person may be exempted from criminal responsibility for an act or omission if he can show that it was done or made in order to avoid consequences which could not otherwise be avoided and which would have inflicted grievous harm or injury on his person, honour or property or on the person or honour of others whom he was bound to protect or on property placed in his charge, provided that he did no more than was reasonably necessary for that purpose and that the harm caused by him was not disproportionate to the harm avoided.

It is highly questionable whether this defence is (or should be) available to a person acting as a public servant. Indeed, there is a clear and specific prohibition against the use of force by such persons contained in section 277 of the same piece of legislation:

> A public servant who does one of the following is liable to imprisonment for three years:

> (1) uses or directs the use of force or violence against a person for the purpose of extorting from him or from anyone in whom he is interested a confession to an offence or information relating to an offence;
>
> (2) threatens any person or directs any person to be threatened, with injury to his person or property or to the person or property of any in whom he is interested for the purpose of extorting from him a confession to an offence or any information relating to an offence.

It is particularly unconscionable to allow a person who is engaged routinely in conduct which lays him or her open to charges of assault or of a breach of section 277 of the Penal Law of 1977 to raise successfully a defence of 'necessity'. Even if it were available, this defence could only apply where the interrogator had committed assault during a 'preventative' interrogation aimed at gathering information on planned future activities. It could not apply to an assault committed during an interrogation of somebody suspected of having already committed an offence, because in that case the 'necessity' of crime prevention would not arise. This important limitation is ignored by the writers of the Report. Instead, they devote a long section to the question of whether the necessity defence is or is not available when the harm to be prevented is not "imminent" (para 3.15). The attempted use of the 'necessity' defence to legitimize the use of psychological and "moderate physical" pressure has been widely criticized by senior Israeli legal academics.[8]

The writers of the Report are at pains to stress that they do not want the image of the Israeli state to resemble "those regimes which grant their security organs unbridled power". (para 3.16) To avoid this, they say, several measures are necessary:

> [F]irst, disproportionate exertion of pressure on the suspect is inadmissible; the pressure must never reach the level of physical torture or maltreatment of the suspect or grievous harm to his honour which deprives him of his human dignity. Second, the possible use of less serious measures must be weighed against the degree of anticipated danger... Third, the physical and psychological means of pressure permitted for use by an interrogator must be defined and limited in advance, by issuing binding directives. Fourth, there must be strict supervision of the implementation in practice of directives given to GSS interrogators. Fifth, the interrogator's superiors must react firmly and without hesitation to any deviation from the permissible... (para 3.15)

In its conclusion, the Report reiterates its finding that "pressure" is an essential ingredient of interrogations of those suspected of "hostile terrorist activity" and that its use is lawful:

> The effective interrogation of terrorist suspects is impossible without the use of means of pressure, in order to overcome an obdurate will not to disclose information and to overcome the fear of the person under interrogation that harm will befall him from his own organization, if he does reveal information.
>
> Interrogation of this kind is permissible under the law, as we interpreted it above, and we think that a confession thus obtained is admissible in a criminal trial, under the existing rulings of the Supreme Court. (para 4.6)

The writers then go on to state that in the secret Appendix to the Report

> We have formulated a code of guidelines for GSS interrogators which define, on the basis of past experience, and with as much precision as possible, the boundaries of what is permitted to the interrogator and mainly what is prohibited to him. (para 4.7)[9]

The implications of the Landau Commission Report

As a document produced by a High Court Judge of a state that purports to be a democracy, the Landau Commission Report is extraordinary. The published recommendations amount to an acceptance that state security can only be maintained if the judiciary countenances convictions based purely on confession evidence obtained by the use of torture, as defined above. This has profound consequences for Palestinians throughout the Occupied Territories, given the widescale criminalization in the name of 'state security' of virtually all forms of political activity undertaken by them.

In addition, the Report creates the extraordinary situation whereby the courts are encouraged to act on recommendations which do not have the force of law. The findings and recommendations of the Commission were adopted by the Knesset on 8 November 1987. However, no legislation was enacted and 'adoption' of a report does not give it the force of law. The clear message to the judiciary from the Knesset, nevertheless, is that the Report is intended to guide them in the future conduct of *voir dire* hearings.

To date, the Israeli judiciary has not been forced to face up to the implications of this politically motivated legal fudging. Should an ex-detainee who had conclusive evidence of having been tortured during interrogation try to prosecute and/or sue his interrogators, the courts might be forced to rule on the legal status of the Report's recommendations, and this pseudo-legal construction might be exposed for what it is.[10] Such a challenge is sadly unlikely because it is extremely rare for a detainee to have conclusive independent evidence of torture, and the fear of very unpleasant repercussions is a strong deterrent to anyone who does have such evidence. (This is discussed further below under the heading 'Complaints, prosecutions and civil actions')

The implication of the Landau Commission Report is that Israel is in flagrant breach of Article 2 of the UN Convention Against Torture, which was quoted earlier (under the heading 'Israel's international obligations not to torture'). The violation of this provision, and of other rules of international law by which Israel is bound, is even more apparent when one examines the influence that the recommendations of the Landau Commission have on a defendant's right to a 'fair and regular trial', discussed in Chapter Three, particularly the conduct of the *voir dire* hearing.

The Influence of Landau on the outcome of the *voir dire*

Since the Landau Commission Report, defence lawyers find themselves in an impossible position. Its authors argue that the courts are entitled to admit in evidence confessions obtained by the use of psychological and "moderate physical" pressure. The implication is that defence lawyers can now only challenge the admissibility of a confession if the pressure used allegedly went beyond this.

Yet the guidelines which lay down what amounts to psychological and "moderate physical" pressure are to remain secret. This makes it particularly difficult to assess the way military judges in security cases approach the test for the admissibility of confessions following the Landau Report. Lawyers who practise in the Israeli military courts differ on the extent to which the Landau Report's recommendation of the use of "moderate physical" pressure has influenced judges. Some say that it has had no practical effect on the way judges approach *voir dire* hearings. Those who believe that it has, say that since Landau, the first question the judge asks himself is "Was physical or psychological abuse used to induce the defendant to confess?" Usually the GSS evidence will be that none was used, and the judge, believing the GSS in preference to the defendant, will answer this question negatively. The judge will then simply rule that the confession was made 'voluntarily' and is therefore admissible. However, sometimes the interrogators giving evidence will admit having used a degree of physical or psychological pressure, such as hooding, and sleep and food deprivation. In this case, the judge will ask himself, "Was the abuse *moderate* ?" as per the language of the Landau Report. The premise seems to be that "moderate" abuse or pressure does not overbear the will, or, in other words, its use is not inconsistent with the confession having been made 'voluntarily'. This, of course, is highly questionable.

It might be thought that since there are no published guidelines as to what is meant by "moderate" in the Report's recommendations, there are no consistent criteria on which individual judges make their assessment of whether a given type of abuse was "moderate" or not. Discussions with practising lawyers suggest one of two possibilities. Either, without reference to any guidelines, judges in security cases simply refuse to believe that any abuse has taken place which goes beyond what they would feel able to call "moderate"; or the judges *have* been supplied with the guidelines in the secret Appendix and are referring to them to determine what is acceptable. Striking evidence of the latter practice was provided by Judge Major Yonatan Livni at a hearing in Dahariya Prison. During a bail application on behalf of Nidal Abu 'Asab, Advocate Nahila 'Atiyah explained that his client had been subjected to torture, including electrical shocks to his stomach and testicles. Judge Livni replied:

> You have nothing to worry about. These things cannot cause the death of the interrogee, and they are also allowed by the Landau Report. I suggest that you try to change the law and procedures.[11]

Whatever criteria the judge employs, once he finds that the abuse in question was "moderate", then he will go on to find that the confession was "free and voluntary".[12]

There can be little doubt that military courts are allowing into evidence confessions which were made as a result of treatment which constitutes torture in international law, whether or not that treatment is authorized by the Landau Commission. Israel is therefore in breach of Article 15 of the UN Convention Against Torture, which requires that:

> Each State Party shall ensure that any statement which is established to have been made as a result of torture shall not be invoked as evidence in any proceedings...

The effective abolition of the 'voluntariness' test by Landau

The Landau Commission argued that Israeli case law on the admissibility of confessions had developed in such a way that confessions made in circumstances which would not enable them to pass the statutory test of 'voluntariness', were nevertheless held to be admissible by judges. In other words, the test for admissibility was supposedly now looser than it originally had been. Therefore, the Report concluded, in order to follow its recommendation on the use of psychological and "moderate physical" pressure during interrogations, no change was required to the law on the admissibility of confessions. This is remarkable. A confession which was made only following the use of "moderate physical" pressure cannot by any stretch of the imagination be said to have been made "freely and voluntarily". If Israeli case law now allows the admission of such confessions, then the statutory test has been stretched out of all recognition.

The significance of removing effective limitations on the admissibility of confession evidence is that it eliminates "a particularly useful deterrent against improper interrogations".[13] It virtually makes holding a *voir dire* a waste of time. By removing an "effective measure" to prevent torture it also constitutes a clear breach of Israel's duties under Article 2 of the UN Convention Against Torture (quoted earlier under the heading 'Israel's international obligations not to torture'). Still, apologists for Israel might point to the right of Palestinians to lodge formal complaints, and the duty of the state in certain circumstances to bring disciplinary or criminal proceedings. There is also the possibility of taking a civil action against the Israeli authorities. Arguably, these could constitute alternative "effective legislative administrative, judicial or other measures" which prevent torture, in partial compliance with Article 2 of the Convention. We now turn to these so-called remedies, in order to assess how successful they are in preventing acts of torture.

Complaints, prosecutions and civil actions

In the case of complaints, prosecutions and civil actions, Israel is under specific legal duties in international law. These duties will be described, and then compared with what happens in practice.

Complaints

Under Article 12 of the UN Convention Against Torture, Israel is required to ensure that its "competent authorities" mount a "prompt and impartial investigation" where there exist "reasonable grounds to believe an act of torture has been committed". Article 13 also requires Israel to ensure that individuals have an effective "right to complain" – with protection from intimidation – leading to prompt and impartial investigation.

In practice Palestinian women are very loath to complain about maltreatment by the GSS, both because they have no faith that their complaint will be upheld and because they fear possible repercussions (such as harassment of themselves and their families by the GSS, police or possibly the army).[14] In the few cases where a complaint is made, it is usually lodged by the woman's lawyer. A letter setting out the allegations is sent either to the Commander of the detention centre (who, as has been explained, is a senior police officer), or to the Prime Minister's office or to the Attorney General. As explained in Chapter One, it is not clear which of these three, if any, is officially responsible for dealing with complaints.[15] When a complaint is received by the Attorney General, he may send the police to investigate or he may tell the GSS to carry out their own internal investigation. This should involve interviewing the woman concerned and those who she says have abused her. A letter should then be sent to the lawyer reporting the result of the investigation. In practice, complaints are very rarely upheld.[16] Often the lawyer does not receive a reply at all; if he or she does, it dismisses the complaint as unfounded. Where the complainant is interviewed, this is sometimes used as an opportunity to subject her to ridicule and/or further abuse. In short, the investigation of complaints is in most cases neither "prompt" nor is it conducted "impartially".

Since complaints have very rarely been upheld in the past, lawyers do not often consider it worthwhile to make them. However, in a case where a detainee has made a confession under pressure, and the detainee instructs her lawyer early on to challenge its admissibility at a *voir dire*, a complaint is sometimes filed purely for tactical reasons. This would be in order to have it on record that the detainee had alleged that she was being maltreated at the first opportunity available to her. It would help to refute any suggestion made by the prosecution at the trial, that she was fabricating allegations of maltreatment in order to have her confession excluded. Still, it would seem that an early complaint to the Israeli authorities will not carry weight with them unless a detainee also complained about her treatment at the first extension of detention hearing, as discussed in Chapter One.[17]

Prosecutions and disciplinary proceedings

Under Article 146 of the Fourth Geneva Convention, Israel is obliged to "seek out and prosecute" anyone alleged to have committed a "grave breach" of the Convention.[18] The list of grave breaches set out in Article 147 includes "torture and inhuman treatment... wilfully causing great suffering or serious injury to body or health", as well as "wilfully depriving a protected person of the rights of fair and regular trial prescribed in the... Convention". In addition, Israel is obliged to "suppress" other breaches of the Convention not amounting to grave breaches, for instance through disciplinary measures. However, in almost all the cases reported in this book concerning "protected persons" grave breaches were committed. (As mentioned earlier, almost all the Palestinians in the Occupied Territories qualify as "protected persons" under the Article 4 of the Fourth Geneva Convention.) Therefore, Israel is under a legal duty to prosecute, rather than simply to discipline, anyone who is "alleged to have committed, or ordered to be committed, such grave breaches". Grave breaches are considered so serious that, under Article 146 of the Convention, if Israel does not prosecute alleged offenders, other states party to the Convention are under a continuing duty to seek out and prosecute them (or extradite them to another state party for trial). We shall return to this duty later.

So far as both "protected" and non-"protected" persons are concerned, Article 4 of the UN Convention Against Torture clearly envisages states prosecuting their own officials involved in committing acts of torture:

> 1. Each State Party shall ensure that all acts of torture are offences under its criminal law. The same shall apply to an attempt to commit torture and to an act by any person which constitutes complicity or participation in torture.
>
> 2. Each State Party shall make these offences punishable by appropriate penalties which take into account their grave nature.

Israel formally complies with its international obligations in this respect, given section 277 of the Penal Law of 1977. Section 277, which was set out in full earlier (under 'Findings and Recommendations of the Landau Commission'), makes it a criminal offence for a public servant to "use or direct the use of force" against an interrogee. Despite this, just as complaints are rarely upheld, so it is almost unheard of for an Israeli official to be prosecuted for a breach of section 277, or for committing any other offence against a detainee. In none of the cases examined in this book was an Israeli GSS officer prosecuted. For that matter, none of the women interviewed or their lawyers were aware of any GSS officer even being disciplined, and it seems most unlikely that any were. The bringing of criminal prosecutions and/or disciplinary proceedings is, as al-Haq has observed, the "most visible test of the state's determination to curb unlawful behaviour on the part of its agents". The experience of practising lawyers and of organizations such as Amnesty International and al-Haq is that Israel almost completely fails this test, so far as acts of torture are concerned.[19]

Civil Actions

Under Article 14 of the UN Convention Against Torture, Israel is required to provide redress to victims of torture through its legal system. In particular, a victim of torture is supposed to have "an enforceable right to adequate compensation". In principle, it is possible to bring an action in the civil courts for assault by a member of the GSS. An ex-detainee wishing to sue for assault would bring her case in the Jerusalem Civil Court. It is thought that this court would accept jurisdiction, even though the woman were a resident of the West Bank or Gaza. (A resident of Jerusalem would obviously have no problem with jurisdiction.) The body to be sued ('the defendant', in legal language) would probably have to be the State of Israel. This is due to the difficulty of identifying an individual GSS officer, and the fact that the GSS report directly to the Prime Minister, rather than to any Ministry. The main problem in winning such an action would be one of evidence.

In trying to produce evidence to prove her case, the woman ('the plaintiff') would encounter all the difficulties referred to in Chapter Three under the heading of 'Proving abuse'. To succeed, she would have to prove that 'on the balance of probabilities' her story of abuse was true. However, if she was able to make out a *prima facie* case that she had been subjected to physical abuse, the lawyers for the defendant might try to raise the 'necessity' defence discussed above. The issues surrounding the necessity defence would then need to be considered. The lawyers acting for the State of Israel would probably try to raise the recommendations in the Landau Commission Report in its defence (ie the recommendation that GSS officers should be allowed to use psychological and "moderate physical" pressure on detainees in interrogation). These do not, of course, have the force of law, so that the court trying the case would first be obliged to make a ruling on the precise legal status of the recommendations. A ruling which effectively endorsed the recommendations of the Landau Commission Report would at least help to clarify matters. The practice of torture documented in this report and elsewhere would then be clearly sanctioned by Israeli law.

In reality, it would probably be impossible for a Palestinian woman to win such an action, and women are very reluctant to bring cases for the same reasons as those which deter them from lodging complaints. Having considered the range of remedies that are theoretically available to detainees and former detainees, it is clear that they do not prevent the practice of torture by GSS officers.

Systematic torture

The stories quoted in this report, although they represent the experiences of a relatively small number of women, suggest that the Israeli practice of torturing female security detainees is widespread. The torture of male Palestinian detainees has been widely documented elsewhere by al-Haq; the Palestine Human Rights Information Centre; B'tselem; the International Commission of Jurists and Amnesty International.[20] Amnesty International describes torture or ill-treatment as appearing to be "virtually institutionalized during the arrest and interrogation procedures".[21] Even more significant are the unusually strong words of the International Committee of the Red Cross (ICRC), restricted as it is by rules of confidentiality, in Press Releases issued in the past two years.[22] The ICRC Press Release of 21 May 1992 is unequivocal:

> By virtue of its mandate under the Fourth Geneva Convention, the ICRC has for many years conducted interviews in private with detainees under interrogation. It has reached the conclusion that to obtain information and confessions from the detainees, means of physical and psychological pressure are being used that constitute a violation of the Convention. Confessions obtained under duress moreover preclude any fair trial.
>
> The ICRC deeply regrets that the numerous and detailed reports it has regularly submitted to the Israeli authorities and its repeated representations at high government level have been to no avail. It has in particular urged the authorities to prohibit all forms of ill-treatment, including insults and threats, to forbid interrogation by co-detainees and the exertion of pressure to induce detainees to collaborate...
>
> ...The Israeli position, which is that security considerations may justify the use of "moderate measures of physical pressure", constitutes in the ICRC's opinion a violation of the relevant provisions of international humanitarian law.
>
> Having observed no substantial or lasting improvement in the situation, the ICRC once again calls on the Government of the State of Israel, which is a party to the Fourth Geneva Convention to ensure that detainees from the occupied territories are duly treated in accordance with the provisions of that Convention.[23]

Following the death in Israeli custody of Mustafa 'Abdallah 'Akkawi on 4 February 1992, al-Haq released the findings of a study it had carried out in the autumn of 1991 which showed that 85% "of a randomly selected pool of 474 detainees were subjected to torture or mistreatment in Israeli custody."[24] Finally, there is strong evidence that Israel and its proxy, the South Lebanon Army, have systematically tortured Lebanese and Palestinian detainees, including many women, held in Khiam Prison, which is situated in Israeli-occupied south Lebanon.[25]

The role of the international community

States which are signatory to the Fourth Geneva Convention of 1949 are under a two-fold duty to intervene where a co-signatory is committing acts of torture in occupied territories. Under Article 1, they are under a general duty to "respect *and ensure respect*" for the terms of the Convention; and under Article 146 they must seek out and prosecute those individuals involved in committing grave breaches, such as torture. States that fail to discharge these obligations are responsible for committing a separate breach of international law.[26]

The duty to "ensure respect" under Article 1

Under this duty, states must act both individually and collectively. Individually, they should take all lawful measures to bring Israel into compliance with the Convention, including the imposition of appropriate conditions on aid, making strenuous diplomatic efforts to have Israel accept the appointment of a "Protecting Power" or even, should these efforts fail, breaking off diplomatic relations. Certainly, it would be a violation of Article 1 for states to render aid or assistance to Israel which might assist it in continuing to breach the Convention.

So far as collective action is concerned, states should first afford mutual assistance to each other in carrying out the above measures, preferably through the United Nations. Ideally, the UN Security Council should then be asked to find a breach of "international peace or security" arising out of Israel's grave breaches of the Fourth Geneva Convention. Under Chapter VII of the UN Charter, the Security Council could then impose conditions on all economic relations between Israel and other member states, ranging from a requirement to "withhold economic intercourse" with Israel to mandatory sanctions backed by a blockade.[27] It could even authorize military intervention to bring about the end of Israeli occupation. The Security Council or the General Assembly of the UN could also ask the International Court of Justice for an advisory opinion on the legality of Israel's activities in the Occupied Territories. (This is not the same as "taking Israel to court" but might embarrass Israel into compliance with international law.)[28]

The duty to prosecute under Article 146

As discussed earlier (under the heading 'Prosecutions and disciplinary proceedings'), Article 146 of the Fourth Geneva Convention requires Israel to prosecute those members of the GSS and other officials who commit grave breaches of the Convention, such as torture. However, states party to the Convention also have clear legal duties to fulfil so far as grave breaches are concerned: they must seek out those individuals concerned and exercise "universal jurisdiction" over them by either prosecuting them in their own courts or extraditing them to co-signatories for trial. This clearly implies the need for states party to the Convention, even those not involved in the Arab-Israeli conflict, to monitor events in the Occupied Territories so as to keep an up-to-date list of suspects for distribution to police and immigration officials at ports of entry. To be done efficiently, this requires co-ordinated inter-state intelligence gathering and distribution, perhaps through the International Criminal Police Organization (Interpol).[29] Articles 5 to 9 of the UN Convention Against Torture make similar provision so far as the prosecution of torturers is concerned.

Few state signatories are currently in a position to be able to prosecute Israeli GSS officers under the grave breaches provisions, because they have failed to enact the necessary domestic legislation. The UK has enacted such legislation, called the Geneva Conventions Act 1957. No prosecutions for grave breaches have taken place to date under that Act.

Notes

1. See Appendix I for a full discussion of the applicability of the Fourth Geneva Convention to Israel's occupation.
2. See Article 18 of the Vienna Convention on the Law of Treaties, 22 May 1969.
3. See Theodor Meron, *Human rights and humanitarian norms as customary law*, 1989, 23. For a short description of customary international law, see Appendix I below.
4. Para 1.6. Quotes are from the English translation of the Landau Commission Report, published by the Government Press Office in October 1987, as reprinted in the *Israel Law Review*, Vol 23, Spring-Summer 1989 Nos. 2–3.
5. Nafsu appealed to the Supreme Court, but before his appeal was heard, the prosecution agreed to ask for the first conviction to be overturned, in exchange for Nafsu agreeing to plead guilty to a lesser charge. His sentence was reduced to two years, and he was released and awarded some financial compensation.
6. One such case is that of Na'ila 'Ayish, described in Chapter Two.
7. The Report never uses the term 'torture' in relation to GSS conduct.

8. See particularly Mordechai Kremnitzer, "The Landau Commission Report – Was the Security Service subordinate to the law, or the law to the needs of the Security Service", *Israel Law Review*, Vol 23, 1989, 216.
9. Indeed, according to Moshe Landau, "The Limits of Pressure", *Israeli Democracy*, 32, at 33, the secret appendix "defines not so much which methods are permitted in interrogations but, rather, which are prohibited." If so, it is very much in line with the public recommendations of Justice Bennett, *Report of the Committee of Inquiry into Police Interrogation Procedures in Northern Ireland* (the Bennett Report), March 1979, para 180.
10. At the time of writing there is a case challenging the legal status and lawfulness of the Report's recommendations pending before the Israeli High Court. One hearing in the case, brought in the name of the Public Committee Against Torture in Israel, took place on 14 April 1992, when the Court decided to adjourn the case pending the completion of the Subcommittee of Special Ministers' "review of directives for interrogators". The Court was advised that this committee, composed of the Ministers of Defence and Justice, was in the process of "retesting the existing directives" See *The Other Front*, Issue No 169, 28 April 1992.
11. *News From Within*, Vol VIII, No 3/4, March-April 1992, 31.
12. It seems that Judges may also consider whether or not the alleged confession makes sense, or is logical, when trying to decide whether or not the confession was 'voluntary'. This test is referred to in the Landau Commission Report, and derives from case law. It is an odd test, since a confession which makes sense could nevertheless have been obtained by methods which mean it was not 'voluntary'.
13. United Nations Department of Economic and Social Affairs, *Study of the right of everyone to be free from arbitrary arrest, detention and exile*, 1964, (E/CN.4/826/Rev.1), para 451.
14 See al-Haq, *A nation under siege*, 1990, 171 and Chapter 16; and B'tselem, *The interrogation of Palestinians during the intifada: ill-treatment*, "moderate physical pressure" or torture?, March 1991, (B'tselem Report), 103104
15. See also B'tselem Report, 103.
16. See B'tselem Report, 8084, where a complaint which was upheld is cited.
17. See Chapter One, under the heading 'Extension of detention hearings'; and Amnesty International, *The military justice system in the Occupied Territories: detention, interrogation and trial procedures*, July 1991, AI index: MDE 15/34/91 (AI Report), 59.
18 For a discussion of the full meaning and implications of Articles 146 and 147 of the Fourth Geneva Convention, see Daniel Machover, *The repression through penal sanctions of grave breaches committed against civilians in occupied territories*, July 1991, LL.M. essay. This essay is on file with Lawyers for Palestinian Human Rights (LPHR).
19. See al-Haq, *A nation under siege*, 1990, 567571; Amnesty International, *Annual Report 1990*, 1990, 131. Although Israel has put members of the security forces on trial on a number of occasions – mostly soldiers who

have killed Palestinians – no case is known where a GSS officer has been tried for torture. Were a decision to be made to prosecute a GSS officer under the criminal law, responsibility for this decision would lie with the Attorney General. For detailed statistics demonstrating the low incidence of prosecutions of Israeli security forces, see al-Haq and Palestine Human Rights Information Centre, *Representation to states signatory to the Fourth Geneva Convention* (and "Supplement" thereto), June 1990.

20. See al-Haq, *A nation under siege*, 1990, 165231; Palestine Human Rights Information Centre, *Israel's Use of Electric Shock Torture in the Interrogation of Palestinian Detainees*, December 1991; B'tselem Report; Report of an ICJ Mission by Jordan J Paust, Gerhard von Glahn and Guenter Woratsch, *Inquiry into the Israeli military court system in the West Bank and Gaza Strip*, 1990, 3233; and the AI Report, 45 et seq.
21. AI Report, 45.
22. See in particular ICRC Press Release No 1675 of 16 July 1991, quoted in footnote 27 of Chapter One; and No 1717 of 21 May 1992.
23. ICRC Press Release No 1717.
24. *al-Haq Alert*, "Torture and death of Palestinians in Israeli custody", 7 February 1992, 2. See also, al-Haq Press Release No 47 of 14 February 1992; Doron Me'iri, "Torture unit", *Hadashot*, 24 February 1992; Richard Beeston, "Israeli police team 'torturing Arabs'", *The Times*, 25 February 1992; and Amnesty International, *Israel and the Occupied Territories: Fear of torture or ill-treatment*, March 1992, AI index: MDE 15/05/92.
25 See Amnesty International, *The Khiam detainees: torture and ill-treatment*, May 1992, AI index: MDE 15/08/92.
26. For detailed discussions of these duties see Marc T Stephens, *Enforcement of international law in the Israeli-Occupied Territories*, al-Haq Occasional Paper No 7, 1989; Labour Middle East Council (LMEC) and Conservative Middle East Council (CMEC), *The enforcement of human rights in the Israeli-Occupied West Bank and Gaza: report of working symposium*; and al-Haq, *A nation under siege*, 1990, 643–667
27. Also, see Stephens, at 3841 & 45, where the possibilities of acting through the UN General Assembly are discussed.
28. See Bill Bowring, *Enforcement of international law -v- interference in internal affairs*, a paper given at a public meeting organized by LPHR, held on 24 June 1992. A copy of this paper is held on file by LPHR.
29. See Daniel Machover, LL.M. essay and LMEC and CMEC, held on file by LPHR.

Appendix I
International Law and the Israeli Occupation of the West Bank & Gaza Strip

Written by Daniel Machover

International Law: Customary and Conventional

The 'law of nations' or 'public international law' is the body of law which governs the relations between states. It also bestows duties and benefits on individuals. Recently it has even granted enforceable rights to individuals, particularly in the field of international human rights law. The main sources of international law are international conventions and international custom.

International Conventions

Conventions, or treaties, are agreements between states. Since they usually take the form of a single written document, treaties are generally a clearer source of international law than custom. With the increase in the number of states, treaties have become increasingly important. This is partly because they are often like contracts between states. Obviously, contracts can be made for a wide variety of purposes. The subjects of these contracts (treaties) could be disputes between states; the establishment of international organizations; or the codification of customary international law.

One of the most important treaties is the Charter of the United Nations, which established the United Nations Organization ('UN' for short) and which nearly all states are party to. The International Court of Justice, or World Court as it is sometimes called, is the most important international court and was set up under part of the UN Charter.

International custom

Customary international law is the body of rules of international law which can be deduced from 'state practice'. For a custom to arise which binds all states there must be a "constant and uniform usage, accepted as law"[1] Controversy rages between international lawyers as to what constitutes 'good evidence' of state practice. However, as indicated above, certain treaties can codify or 'be declaratory of' customary international law.

International Humanitarian Law and International Human Rights Law

During the course of this report, repeated reference is made to one particular treaty, the Fourth Geneva Convention of 1949. Its terms provide the main legal yardstick under international law against which to measure Israeli policies and practices in the West Bank and Gaza Strip.

International humanitarian law and the four Geneva Conventions of 1949

The term 'international humanitarian law' refers to a range of international legal provisions, arising from both customary law and treaties, which seek to ensure respect for the individual in armed conflict. International treaties in this field date back to the Geneva Convention of 1864 (on the wounded and sick), which established the role of the International Committee of the Red Cross.

After the Second World War, a number of international conferences took place with the purpose of drafting revisions to previous conventions on the law of war. This process culminated in the convening of a large diplomatic conference in Geneva on 21 April 1949. The conference produced the four Geneva Conventions of 12 August 1949, containing a total of 429 Articles. Today, the signatories to the Conventions outnumber the member states of the United Nations.

The full title of the fourth Convention is the Geneva Convention Relative to the Protection of Civilian Persons in Time of War of 12 August 1949. This Convention, together with the Regulations annexed to the Fourth Hague Convention of 18 October 1907, constitute the law governing 'belligerent occupation'. Before explaining why the law on belligerent occupation, particularly the Fourth Geneva Convention, is applicable to Israel's occupation of the West Bank and Gaza Strip, it is helpful to distinguish between international humanitarian law and human rights law

International Human Rights Law

The international law of human rights is a separate branch of international law from international humanitarian law, although the two areas do overlap and have the same central purpose: the protection of human beings. As explained above, international humanitarian law is a part of the law of armed conflict, and it seeks to protect individuals not taking part in the conflict at all, or who have been placed *hors de combat*, so as to ensure that they are treated humanely. By contrast, historically human rights law, whether purely domestic (eg the Habeas Corpus Act of 1679) or international (eg The International Covenant on Civil and Political Rights of 1966) is primarily concerned with the relations between states and their own nationals in time of peace.

However, all the major international conventions on human rights concluded since the Second World War contain provisions for their implementation in time of war or "public emergency threatening the life of the nation", with certain rights being 'non-derogable'. That is, certain human rights must be respected by states signatory to those conventions even during time of war, including the right of everyone not to be tortured.

Indeed, special rules apply even to those rights which are 'derogable' in that a state is only supposed to breach those provisions "to the extent strictly required by the exigencies of the situation". Therefore, international humanitarian law treaties such as the Geneva Conventions can be applicable in the same place and at the same time as at least certain provisions of international human rights treaties such as the ICCPR. This is precisely the position that now exists in the Israeli-Occupied Territories.

The applicability of the Fourth Geneva Convention to the Israeli Occupation

Israel does not accept that the Fourth Geneva Convention of 1949 is applicable to its occupation of the West Bank and Gaza Strip.

Israeli arguments concerning the applicability of the Fourth Geneva Convention are based mainly upon an unsupported reading of Article 2 of the Convention (and also on a failure to acknowledge the significance of Article 4).

Article 2 states:

> ...the present Convention shall apply to all cases of declared war or of any other armed conflict which may arise between two or more High Contracting Parties, even if the state of war is not recognized by one of them.
>
> The Convention shall also apply to all cases of partial or total occupation of the territory of a High Contracting Party, even if the said occupation meets with no armed resistance.

Israeli jurists argue that the second paragraph means that the Convention *only* applies to occupation by one HCP of territory legitimately held previously by another HCP and, so the argument continues, neither Jordan nor Egypt having ever been the legitimate sovereigns of the West Bank or Gaza Strip respectively, it is excluded from applying to those territories.[2]

World legal opinion and other High Contracting Parties have not accepted Israeli arguments about the inapplicability of the Fourth Geneva Convention. The internationally accepted position is that the Convention is applicable, for the following reasons:

1. Article 2 provides that the Convention shall apply to all cases of declared war or of any other armed conflict between signatories. (All states in the region are signatories of the Convention.)

2. The Convention is not intended to exclude those situations where title to a given territory is disputed.

3. Under Article 4, the Convention sought to protect all people who find themselves in the hands of an Occupying Power of which they are not nationals.

The USA has repeatedly stated its unequivocal position:

a) On 1 July 1969 the US official at the UN Security Council stated that Israel was required by law to apply the Fourth Geneva Convention; he added that the US has "so informed the Government of Israel on numerous occasions since July 1967."[3]

b) On 4 February 1978 the US joined a UN Commission on Human Rights (Economic and Social Council) consensus resolution which deplored the failure of Israel to acknowledge the applicability of the Fourth Geneva Convention.[4]

Meanwhile, in the UK, the position of Her Majesty's Government is equally clear and was recently summarized by the Rt Hon William Waldegrave MP, the then Minister of State at the Foreign Office, as follows:

> The Israeli government is well aware that the international community, including this Government, consider the Fourth Geneva Convention to be applicable to the Occupied Territories.[5]

An Overview of the Provisions of the Fourth Geneva Convention

The Convention contains 159 Articles and two Annexes. The draft Preamble proposed by the French and Finnish Delegations said that the Convention was designed to "ensure the respect of human personality and dignity by putting beyond reach of attack those rights and liberties which are the essence of existence." The Convention is divided into four Parts.

Part I of the Convention

Part I (Article 1 to 12) contains the General Provisions. As indicated earlier, Article 4 is particularly significant, because it defines those to whom the Convention applies ("protected persons") so as to include people who find themselves in the hands of an Occupying Power of which they are not nationals. Clearly, the Palestinian residents of the Occupied Territories fall into this category.

Part II of the Convention

Part II (Article 13 to 26) concerns the general protection of populations against the different consequences of war. These provisions have a wider application than the rest of the Convention, as they cover the population as a whole, including those who are nationals of the Occupying Power. Provision is made for hospital and safety zones and localities, and neutralized zones (Article 14 & 15), for the protection of civilian hospitals (Article 18), and for the exchange of family news (Article 25).

Part III of the Convention

Part III (Article 27 to 141) defines the status and treatment of protected persons (ie those defined in Article 4), and the manner of the application of the Convention. It is divided into five sections.

Section I deals with the responsibilities of the State and of its agents (Article 29), prohibits corporal punishments (Article 32), collective penalties, terrorism, pillage and reprisals (Article 33), and the taking of hostages (Article 34). Despite the Article 33 prohibition of collective penalties, repeatedly breached by Israel in the past 25 years, former Israeli Justice Minister Dan Meridor justified such measures as being necessary to "win the war against the *intifada*."[6]

Section II relates to aliens in the territory of a Party to the conflict and is of little interest for our purposes. On the other hand, Section III is extremely important in the context of the West Bank and Gaza Strip. It contains the prescriptions for occupied territories on such crucial subjects as the inviolability of rights (Article 47), deportations and transfers (absolutely prohibited) and evacuations (Article 49), children (Article 50), labour (Article 51), food (Article 55), hygiene and public health (Article 56), penal legislation including the right to a regular trial and to unimpeded legal assistance in the preparation of a defence (Article 64 to 75: See Appendix II below), and the treatment of prisoners held awaiting trial (Article 76). Article 78 sanctions the use of assigned residence and internment (ie administrative detention in the Israeli context) only where necessary for imperative reasons of security.

Section IV is itself divided into twelve chapters, containing a total of 56 Articles, laying down detailed regulations governing the treatment of internees. The Convention recognizes that as internees face no formal charge or trial, they are entitled to more privileged treatment than ordinary prisoners. The provisions are in general analogous to those adopted for prisoners of war and cover such matters as the location and general conditions of internment camps (Chap II), food and clothing (Chap III), hygiene and medical attention (Chap IV), religious, intellectual and physical activities (Chap V), and administration and discipline (Chap VII).

Section V is concerned with the establishment and functioning of Information Bureaux and the Central Information Agency.

Part IV of the Convention

Part IV (Article 142 to 159) is devoted to the execution of the Convention. Articles 146 to 149 are particularly significant. They govern the repression of breaches of the Convention. Article 146 imposes penal sanctions for such breaches, particularly grave breaches, as defined in the succeeding Article. Grave breaches include wilful killing, torture, deportation, unlawful confinement and wilfully depriving a protected person of the rights to a fair and regular trial.

The Relevant Provisions of the Convention

While disputing the applicability of the Fourth Geneva Convention to its occupation of the West Bank and Gaza Strip, Israel claims to adhere to the "humanitarian" provisions of the Convention, on a voluntary basis. However, Israel has never indicated precisely which of the provisions of the Convention it regards as "humanitarian". It is difficult to see how the provisions of the Convention which forbid torture could be regarded as other than "humanitarian".

The following are some of the provisions of the Convention which have the greatest relevance to the subject matter of this report. It will be noticed that, if the allegations made by the women interviewed for the report are true, Israel breaches these provisions regularly.

1. Articles 27, 31 and 32 are general, that is, they do not specifically deal with the conduct of criminal investigations or legal proceedings, but they can be applied to them.

Article 27

> Protected persons are entitled, in all circumstances, to respect for their persons, their honour, their family rights, their religious convictions and practices, and their manners and customs. They shall at all times be humanely treated, and shall be protected especially against all acts of violence or threats thereof and against insults and public curiosity.
>
> Women shall be especially protected against any attack on their honour, in particular against rape, enforced prostitution, or any form of indecent assault.

Article 31

> No physical or moral coercion shall be exercised against protected persons, in particular to obtain information from them or from third parties.

Article 32

> The High Contracting Parties specifically agree that each of them is prohibited from taking any measure of such a character as to cause the physical suffering or extermination of protected persons in their hands. This prohibition applies not only to murder, torture, corporal punishment, mutilation and medical or scientific experiments not necessitated by the medical treatment of a protected person, but also to any other measures of brutality whether applied by civilian or military agents.

2. Articles 64 to 76 specifically apply to people subject to penal proceedings and most of these provisions are discussed separately in Appendix II. However, the following provisions are also relevant:

Article 37

Protected persons who are confined pending proceedings or serving a sentence involving loss of liberty, shall during their confinement be humanely treated.

Article 76

Protected persons accused of offences shall be detained in the occupied country, and if convicted they shall serve their sentences therein. They shall, if possible, be separated from other detainees and shall enjoy conditions of food and hygiene which will be sufficient to keep them in good health, and which will be at least equal to those obtaining in prisons in the occupied country.

They shall receive the medical attention required by their state of health.

They shall also have the right to receive any spiritual assistance which they may require.

Women shall be confined in separate quarters and shall be under the direct supervision of women.

Proper regard shall be paid to the special treatment due to minors.

Protected persons who are detained shall have the right to be visited by delegates of the Protecting Power and of the International Committee of the Red Cross, in accordance with the provisions of Article 143.

Such persons shall have the right to receive at least one relief parcel monthly.

3. Finally, Articles 16 and 81 are quoted because they are of relevance to the pregnancy cases discussed in Appendix II. Article 16 is of general application, and Article 81 applies to Administrative Detainees.

Article 16

The wounded and sick, as well as the infirm, and expectant mothers, shall be the object of particular protection and respect.

Article 81

Parties to the conflict who intern protected persons shall be bound to provide free of charge for their maintenance, and to grant them also the medical attention required by their state of health.

Notes

1. The quotation is from the judgment of the International Court of Justice, in the case of *Columbia* -v- *Peru*, also known as "The Asylum Case", *ICJ Reports* 1950, 266.

2. See Shamgar, "The observance of international law in the administered territories", *Israel Yearbook on Human Rights*, Vol 1, 1971, 262; T.S. Kuttner, "Israel and the West Bank: aspects of the law of belligerent occupation", *Israel Yearbook on Human Rights*, Vol 7, 1977, 166, at 168181; B. Farhy, "Current legal trends in the areas administered by Israel", *Military Law Review*, at 50. The latter was the Military Advocate General of the day. The argument does not apply to the occupation of the Golan Heights, which is therefore governed by the terms of the Convention, as were the 15 year Israeli occupation of Sinai and the two Israeli occupations of southern Lebanon. As to the latter, see: A. Roberts, "Prolonged military occupation: the Israeli-occupied territories since 1967", *American Journal of International Law*, Vol 84, 1990, 44, at 60. The general legal position in the Sinai, Golan Heights and Lebanon respectively will not be further examined.
3. 61 *Department of State Bulletin* 76, 28 July 1969.
4. See Roberts, op cit, at 6970.
5. Letter to LPHR and the Haldane Society of Socialist Lawyers, 13 June 1989.
6. *Jerusalem Post International Edition*, 7 October 1989.

Appendix II
The Right to a 'fair and regular trial'

Written by Daniel Machover

As was explained at the beginning of Chapter Three, the right to a fair and regular trial is of crucial importance in international humanitarian law. This appendix explains the content of this right, so far as civilians in occupied territories are concerned. It will be recalled that Article 71 of the Fourth Geneva Convention 1949 (see Appendix I) provides a general rule:

> No sentence shall be pronounced by the competent courts of the Occupying Power except after a regular trial.
>
> Accused persons who are prosecuted by the Occupying Power shall be promptly informed, in writing, in a language which they understand, of the particulars of the charges preferred against them, and shall be brought to trial as rapidly as possible. The Protecting Power shall be informed of all proceedings instituted by the Occupying Power against protected persons in respect of charges involving the death penalty or imprisonment for two years or more; it shall be enabled, at any time, to obtain information regarding the state of such proceedings. Furthermore, the Protecting Power shall be entitled, on request, to be furnished with all particulars of these and of any other proceedings instituted by the Occupying Power against protected persons.
>
> The notification to the Protecting Power, as provided for in the second paragraph above, shall be sent immediately, and shall in any case reach the Protecting Power three weeks before the date of the first hearing. Unless, at the opening of the trial, evidence is submitted that the provisions of this Article are fully complied with, the trial shall not proceed. The notification shall include the following particulars:
>
> (a) description of the accused;
> (b) place of residence or detention;
> (c) specification of the charge or charges (with mention of the penal provisions under which it is brought);
> (d) designation of the court which will hear the case;
> (e) place and date of the first hearing.

Article 72 provides:

> Accused persons shall have the right to present evidence necessary to their defence and may, in particular, call witnesses. They shall have the right to be assisted by a qualified advocate or counsel of their own choice, who shall be able to visit them freely and shall enjoy the necessary facilities for preparing the defence.
>
> Failing a choice by the accused, the Protecting Power may provide him with an advocate or counsel. When an accused person has to meet a serious charge and the Protecting Power is not functioning, the Occupying Power, subject to the consent of the accused, shall provide an advocate or counsel.
>
> Accused persons shall, unless they freely waive such assistance, be aided by an interpreter, both during preliminary investigation and during the hearing in court. They shall have the right at any time to object to the interpreter and to ask for his replacement.
>
> However, it is important to place Articles 71 and 72 in the context of a broader array of what are sometimes collectively called "due process guarantees". It is not generally appreciated that, as a general rule, Article 64 of the Fourth Geneva Convention requires that "all legal provisions in connection with the repression of offences" remain in force in the Occupied Territories and "must be respected by the Occupying Power"[1], and that local Palestinian criminal courts "shall continue to function in respect of all offences covered by the said laws."

Article 64 only permits the military authorities to enact criminal laws in limited circumstances. Such laws must, for example, be essential to "maintain the orderly government of the territor[ies], and to ensure the security of the Occupying Power, [and] of the members and property of the occupying forces or administration." Although this still allows Israel considerable leeway, it is clear that "these varied measures must not under any circumstances serve as a means for oppressing the population."[2]

Moreover, even where the Israeli authorities are permitted to pass Military Orders amending or supplementing local criminal law, Article 65 requires that such Orders cannot have retroactive effect and do not even come into force until they have been "published and brought to the knowledge" of the inhabitants of the West Bank and Gaza Strip in Arabic. Thus, no lawful, let alone 'fair and regular', trial of a Palestinian from the Occupied Territories by Israeli military courts is possible unless Articles 64 and 65 have first been complied with.

Meanwhile, under Article 66, women (or men) accused of committing offences in breach of Military Orders which comply with Articles 64 and 65 of the Convention may only be "handed over" from local Palestinian criminal jurisdiction to Israel's "properly constituted, non-political military courts", which must themselves sit in the Occupied Territories.

From this rule it is clear that an Israeli military court should not:

(a) hear a case unless the Military Order invoked fully complies with Articles 64 and 65; or

(b) try any ordinary criminal case, involving a breach of the pre-1967 criminal law (eg a murder charge not involving the death of a member of the Israeli army or administration), which should instead be heard by the local criminal court.

Second, where these jurisdictional requirements are met, only "ordinary" Israeli military courts are "competent" to hear such cases (ie the same courts which try Israeli soldiers for offences committed in the Occupied Territories). According to Dr. Pictet, the fact that such courts must be "non-political" constitutes a prohibition on "certain practices resorted to during the Second World War when the judicial machinery was sometimes used as an instrument of political or racial persecution."[3] By the criminalization under Military Orders of many purely political activities, Israel has clearly breached this prohibition.[4]

Therefore, returning to the Article 71 "regular trial" requirement, no trial before an Israeli military court can be "regular" unless the provisions of Articles 64–66 inclusive have first been met. Dr. Pictet makes this point:

> The safeguards provided in the Articles dealing with penal legislation..., and those prescribed elsewhere, particularly in Article 32, which prohibits torture and all other forms of brutality, obviously represent conditions which must be fulfilled if a trial is to be regular.[5]

Moreover, as these words make clear, the right to a 'regular trial' encompasses the protection of the defendant's rights from the time of arrest to the conclusion of the trial.

In drawing up a list of fair trial rights, one can properly rely on specific rights which appear in Article 75 of Geneva Protocol I Additional to the Geneva Conventions of 1949, and Relating to the Protection of Victims of International Armed Conflicts of 10 June 1977, as well as those rights which have already been mentioned and the rights which appear in Articles 71 and 72 of the Fourth Geneva Convention. Put simply, although Israel is not a party to that Protocol, Article 75 is widely considered, including by US Government experts, to be declaratory of customary humanitarian (and possibly human rights) law and therefore binding on Israel in any event.[6]

In addition, one can rely on certain due process-related 'non-derogable' human rights (ie those that a state is not permitted to breach even in times of war or national emergency) which appear in treaties Israel has ratified (ie agreed to be legally bound by), including the ICCPR and UNCAT. Thus, under international humanitarian law and under international human rights law, every Palestinian woman from the West Bank and Gaza Strip is entitled to the following minimum due process and fair trial rights (ie even if Israel claims that there exists in those territories a "war or other national emergency threatening the life of the nation"):

1. The right not to be arrested under a Military Order which does not comply with the provisions of Articles 64 and 65 of the Fourth Geneva Convention.

2. The right to be "promptly informed, in writing, in a language which [she] understands [ie Arabic], of the particulars of the charges preferred" against her.[7]

3. The right

(a) not to be subjected to "physical or moral coercion...in particular to obtain information from [her] or from third parties"; and not to be subjected to "any measure of such a character as to cause...physical suffering", including torture and "any other measures of brutality whether applied by civilian or military agents";[8] and

(b) the concomitant right not to be "compelled to testify against oneself or to confess guilt".[9]

4. The right to be "brought to trial as rapidly as possible".[10]

5. Where it is lawful for the trial not to be held before the ordinary Palestinian courts, the right to be tried by Israel's "properly constituted, non-political military courts".[11]

6. The right to be presumed innocent until proved guilty.[12]

7. The right to "all necessary rights and means of defence".[13] More particularly:

(a) The right to "present evidence necessary to [her] defence...and call witnesses";[14] and

(b) The right to be "assisted by a qualified advocate or counsel of [her] own choice, who shall be able to visit [her] freely and shall enjoy the necessary facilities for preparing the defence".[15]

8. The right to be present at trial.[16]

9. The right to be "aided by an interpreter, both during the preliminary investigation and during the hearing in court" and the right "at any time to object to the interpreter and to ask for his replacement".[17]

Notes

1. Pictet etc, 335 (commentary on the first paragraph of Article 64).
2. Ibid, 337 (commentary on the second paragraph of Article 64).
3. Ibid, 340 (commentary on Article 66).

4. An early example is Military Order No. 101 of 27 August 1967. See Raja Shehadeh and Jonathan Kuttab, *The West Bank and the Rule of Law*, 1980, 126128, for the full text of this Order (as amended by Military Order No.718). The authors observe (at 82) that the order, inter alia, "prohibits the gathering or convening without permit of ten or more people for a march or a meeting where it is possible to hear a speech on a subject which may be considered political."
5. Pictet, 353 (commentary on the first paragraph of Article 71).
6. See Theodor Meron, *Human Rights and Humanitarian Norms as Customary International Law*, 1990, (Meron), 68 & 9697; Jaime Oraa, *Human Rights in a State of Emergency in International Law*, 1992, (Oraa) 114–124; and Stephanos Stavros, "*The right to a fair trial in Emergency Situations*", International and Comparative Law Quarterly, Vol. 41, 1992, (Stavros) 343, at 351 et seq.

The fact that various "fair trial" or "due process" rights are "non-derogable" (ie states are not allowed to breach them) in time of war provides some evidence that a certain "core" of such rights are non-derogable under international human rights law, despite the fact that the international treaties in this field do not make them so. Oraa, 114–124; Stavros, 343.

The list of rights set out in the text accompanying notes 717 below is similar to that set out by Oraa, at 115–116.

7. See the second paragraph of Article 71 of the Fourth Geneva Convention.
8. See Articles 31 & 32 of the Convention; Article 1 of the United Nations Convention Against Torture 1984 (UNCAT) and Article 7 of the International Convention on Civil and Political Rights (ICCPR).
9. Articles 32 and 71 of the Convention read together and Article 75(4)(f) of Protocol I, as well as Articles 7 and 14(3)(g) of the ICCPR read together.
10. See the second paragraph of Article 71 of the Convention.
11. See Article 66 of the Convention and Article 75 (4) of Protocol I.
12. According to Pictet (at 354) this right follows "logically" from the first paragraph of Article 71. Also, see Article 75(4)(d) of Protocol I and Article 14 (2) of the ICCPR.
13. See Article 75(4)(a) of Protocol I and Article 7(3)(b) of the ICCPR.
14. See the first paragraph of Article 72 of the Convention, Article 75(4)(g) of Protocol I and Article 14(3)(e) of the ICCPR.
15. See the first paragraph of Article 72 of the Convention.
16. See Article 75(4)(e) of Protocol I.
17. See the third paragraph of Article 72 of the Convention.

Appendix III
Background Information on Women Interviewed for the Report

Group I – Palestinian Women from the West Bank, Gaza and East Jerusalem

Ra'ida al-'Ataba from Nablus. Single. Age 23 when arrested on 25 July 1990. Interrogated for 36 hours in Jalama. Confessed. Charged with organising for an illegal organization. Sentenced to one year and four months in prison. (Quotes are from affidavit taken by lawyer Salma Wakim and published by Sanabel Press Services, Jerusalem.)

Na'ila 'Ayish, from Gaza. Married, one child. Age 26 when arrested on 19 February 1987. Interrogated for 9 days in the Russian Compound. Confessed. Charged with membership of an illegal organization and rendering services to that organization. Prepared to challenge the admissibility of her confession at trial, but withdrew and was sentenced under a plea bargain to a suspended prison term.

Fatma Abu Bakra, from Gaza. Widowed, two children. Age about 30 when arrested on 23 November 1986. Interrogated for 50 days in Ashkelon prison. Confessed. Charged with membership of an illegal organization and another offence (unknown). Prepared to challenge the admissibility of her confession at trial, but withdrew and agreed to be sentenced under a plea bargain. The prosecution asked for five years but the judge gave her seven years, which was then reduced on appeal to six years. Currently a serving prisoner in Tel Mond prison. (Quotes are from affidavit taken by her lawyer, Leah Tsemel.)

Salwa Abu Hani, from the West Bank. Married, two children. Age 26 when arrested on 27 September 1987. Interrogated for 17 days in Jalama and the Russian Compound. Did not confess. Released without charge. Had been detained previously.

Ikram Abu Sbih, from Jerusalem. Single. Age 17 when arrested 3 July 1988. Interrogated for 27 days in the Russian Compound. Charge not known. Sentenced to seven months' imprisonment plus a fine of NIS 3000 (about £800) and banned from travelling abroad for three years.

Ghalia Abu Samra, from Gaza. Married, six children. Age 32 when arrested 7 November 1989. Interrogated for 15 days in Gaza military centre and Ashkelon prison. Confessed. Charged with providing arms, distributing funds and smuggling letters out of prison. Sentenced to five and a half months' imprisonment plus a suspended sentence of two and a half years and a fine of NIS 3000.

Terry Boullata, a human rights worker from Jerusalem. Single when detained. Now married with one child. Age 21 when arrested 4 November 1987. Interrogated for 18 days in the Russian Compound. Did not confess. Charged with membership of an illegal organization. Sentenced to two months' immediate imprisonment plus a three year suspended sentence. Had been detained previously.

Iman Jadallah, a civil engineer from Jerusalem. Single. Age 27 when arrested on 24 July 1990. Interrogated for about 11 days, in the Russian Compound. Confessed. Charge not known. Sentenced to one year and eight months' immediate imprisonment plus a suspended sentence of one year and eight months. (Quotes are from affidavit taken by lawyer, Hiyam Qarawani and published by Sanabel Press Services.)

Maha Nassar from Jerusalem, a physics teacher. Married with three children. Age 33 when arrested 17 July 1988. Interrogated for 11 days in the Russian Compound. Did not confess and was released without charge. Arrested again on 4 October 1989. Interrogated for 13 days in the Russian Compound. Did not confess and was released without charge. (Several other periods in detention.)

Fatma Salama, from Nablus. Single. Age 28 when arrested on 25 July 1990. Interrogated for two days in Jalama. Confessed. Charged with membership of an illegal organization. Sentenced to one year and two months' imprisonment. (Quotes are from affidavit taken by lawyer, Salma Wakim and published by Sanabel Press Services.)

Suha Sanduqa, a school student from Jerusalem. Age 14 when arrested on 16 June 1989. Taken to the Qishlah police station in Jerusalem, released later that day. Charged with insulting a policeman. Given a five months' suspended prison sentence and a suspended fine of NIS 500. Arrested again on 26 February 1990, now aged 15. Taken to the Russian Compound. Interrogated for one day. Did not confess. Charged with throwing a stone at a bus. Sentenced to eight months' imprisonment.

Group II – Palestinian Israeli Women

Kifah Kayal, a student and journalist from Acre. Single. Age 24 when arrested on 9 August 1988. Interrogated for 53 days, mainly in Jalama but transferred on several occasions (to the Russian Compound, Abu Kabir and Ashkelon.) Did not confess. Charge not known. Granted bail in March 1989. Still awaiting trial. (Had been detained previously.)

Hanan Rahim, a newspaper clerk from Shefa'amr, near Haifa. Single. Age 29 when arrested on 17 December 1989. Interrogated for 9 days in Jalama. Did not confess. Released without charge.

Maryam Qadumi, a nurse from Shefa'amr, near Haifa. Single. Age 19 when arrested on 15 June 1990. Interrogated for 13 days in Jalama. Did not confess. Charged with membership in an illegal organization and other matters. Released on bail. Outcome of trial not known.

Group III – Jewish Israeli Women

Roni Ben Efrat, a journalist and peace activist from Jerusalem.

Two children. Age 36 when arrested on 24 April 1988. Interrogated for approximately 25 days, in Petakh Tikva police station. Confessed. Charged with membership in an illegal organization and performing services for such an organization. Challenged the admissibility of her confession at trial. Trial collapsed into a plea bargain. Sentenced to nine months' imprisonment.

Michal Schwartz, a journalist and peace activist from Jerusalem. Two children. Age 39 when arrested on 27 April 1990. Interrogated for 20 days in Petakh Tikva police station. Confessed. Charged with membership in an illegal organization and performing services for such an organization. Challenged the admissibility of her confession at trial. Trial collapsed into a plea bargain. Sentenced to eighteen months' imprisonment.

Appendix IV
Miscarriages Brought on by Maltreatment in Prison and Detention

During the research done in the preparation of this report, three cases came to light in which a woman who had been pregnant when arrested, subsequently miscarried. In all three cases the miscarriage was apparently brought on partly or wholly as a result of maltreatment and or medical neglect whilst in prison or GSS custody. In a fourth case, it appears that GSS officers tried to cause a woman to miscarry, but were unsuccessful.

It was decided to document these cases and include them in this report because they illustrate a unique problem faced by women in custody, which has not been documented elsewhere and which involves an exceptionally serious human rights abuse. What follows, however, is a series of case histories rather than a comprehensive study of the problem.

Of the three women who miscarried, Tahani Abu Daqqa was in administrative detention in Ramla prison at the time; Na'ila 'Ayish was under interrogation by the GSS in the Russian Compound in Jerusalem, and Widad Darwish had just been released from a twenty-four hour period of GSS interrogation in the Russian Compound, following her arrest and beating by Border Guards. The fourth case is that of 'Ayisha al-Kurd, who was interrogated by GSS officers in Gaza prison and then taken to Ashkelon prison. She did not miscarry.

It is usually very difficult to establish conclusively what has caused a miscarriage. Stress is recognized as an important factor, and no doubt for some women the fact of being under arrest would in itself be sufficient to bring on a miscarriage.

It may be said, however, that in the three cases of miscarriage described below, it seems very probable that the treatment to which the women were subjected whilst in custody was a major if not the sole cause.

Case Summaries

1. Tahani Suliman Abu Daqqa

Tahani Abu Daqqa, from Gaza, was President of the Gaza section of the Palestinian Federation of Women's Action Committees in 1990.

(The statement is based on an affidavit taken by al-Haq and quoted with their permission (al-Haq affidavit number 1528), and on two interviews with Tahani Suliman Abu Daqqa conducted by the author.)

2. On 3 May 1988 I was arrested from my home at the above address and placed under administrative detention. Three other women from Gaza were arrested at the same time as me. We were the first women from Gaza to be placed under administrative detention during the *intifada*. We were taken to Ramla prison in Israel and held with other Palestinian women political prisoners.

3. My daughter Maryam was ten months old at the time of my arrest and I requested that she be allowed to join me. Twenty days after I made the request, permission was given. I was placed in a cell by myself. It was kept locked all the time. After one week my daughter was brought to me.

4. From then on I shared the cell with her and another prisoner, 'Ayisha al-Kurd, who was eight months pregnant. We were obliged to take our meals in the room, but we were allowed to go out whenever we needed to. However, we were not permitted to associate with the other Palestinian prisoners, but only with the Israeli women prisoners. Since I had previously been attacked by some Israeli prisoners, I did not go out of the cell. We lived like this for about ten days.

5. In mid-May I asked the prison nurse to do a pregnancy test for me, as I believed I might be pregnant. I gave a urine sample, and ten days later I was told that the result was positive. By this time I was feeling increasingly tired.

6. The prison clinic told me that I should have an abortion. I refused. They told me that I did not appear happy when they told me that I was pregnant. I explained that I did not like the idea of undergoing a pregnancy in prison. I also said that my religion does not permit abortion and added that I, myself, did not want to have an abortion.

7. The next time my husband came to visit me, not knowing that I was pregnant, the prison director sent for me. She told my husband, in my presence, that I was pregnant. She offered to help to arrange an abortion, saying that we would regret it if we refused, but I told her that I did not want to have an abortion.

8. The director then said that my administrative detention order would be renewed and that my daughter who was with me in prison was still small and needed care. My husband and I told her that we were prepared to send our daughter back home, and that I would go back to the room with the rest of the women political prisoners.

9. I had to wait a week for one of these prisoners to be released, as there was no place available. My daughter remained with me for that week and then returned home.

10. When lawyer Leah Tsemel visited me, I told her that my health was deteriorating because of the pregnancy and lack of medical care. She spoke with the prison administration asking them to improve the situation and offer the necessary medical treatment.

11. After this, a nurse in a white uniform came to see me and asked about my health; I told her that I felt dizzy and that I was vomiting. I told her that I needed a complete examination, but she started shouting saying: "You should put up with it, if you wanted to get pregnant; why did you get pregnant if you are unable to endure it? You people are only good for having children and writing about us in the newspapers!"

12. The nurse then took a blood sample from me, about two and a half cubic centimetres, but she did not inform me of the results of the test.

13. My daughter was taken away and sent to the family and I was left alone in the room. I was locked in for 24 hours, without a break. Food was brought to me in the room and in general it was not bad, but my psychological condition was very bad.

14. Two weeks after the blood was taken, the nurse came and told me that I was suffering from inflammation in the urinary tract and that I should take some tablets. She had brought a handful of them without any packet or box to enable me to see what they contained. She told me to take two in the morning and two in the evening but I was afraid to take them.

15. I heard from an Arab Israeli woman prisoner that when she had an allergy in her foot, she was given some tablets. Later, she found out that they were the same tablets that were given to drug addicts. Therefore I talked to a drug addict prisoner, from behind the door, and told her about my reluctance to take the tablets. This prisoner informed the prison officer that I was not taking the tablets. The prison officer came and told me that the foetus would be damaged if I did not take the tablets, which were white in colour.

16. I agreed to take the tablets for a week, whilst I remained alone in the room where I had been with my daughter.

17. On a Thursday, I was taken to the room with the rest of the political prisoners. On Saturday, two days later, the nurse sent for me and asked to take another blood sample. I protested that she had taken two samples but had not shown me the results. She said that the first sample was taken in order to make sure that I was in good health, and that this time they wanted to find out whether my body would be able to cope with the "abortion". I told her that I did not want an abortion and that my husband had refused when the prison director had suggested it. But the nurse said, while she was taking the blood, "It is not a question of what you or your husband want!" which seemed to mean that I was going to be made to have an abortion against my will.

18. I went back to the room. In the morning of the next day I found that I was bleeding. I went to the clinic, where the nurse told me that the bleeding was not serious and there was no need to worry.

The bleeding got more serious in the afternoon and I was handcuffed and taken in the prison car to Sarafand hospital.

19. When we arrived at the hospital, I was made to walk a long way from one section to another. It is a very large hospital and cars are used to go from one section to another. I was taken up and down flights of stairs and made to walk from one place to another, although other women in a similar condition were carried on stretchers. A male and a female soldier accompanied me.

20. The doctor examined me and told me that there was a fifty per cent chance that the foetus was dead. He then said, in front of the woman soldier, that I could return to prison, but that if I started to bleed again and there were blood clots, I should go back to the hospital as soon as possible or my life would be endangered. The doctor spoke in Hebrew and the soldiers translated into Arabic.

21. I wish to add that we left the prison to go to the hospital at 5pm and left the hospital at 9pm. At midnight, back in the prison, the bleeding got more serious and I called the prison officer and told her that there were clots in the blood and that according to the doctor's instructions, I should go to the hospital. She told me that I could not leave the prison until the morning and then I called the officer in charge and explained the situation to her. She refused to take me to hospital and insisted on waiting till the morning before taking me there. I waited until morning, in pain.

22. It is important to mention that I was not provided with sanitary towels. I either used paper napkins or borrowed towels which other prisoners had bought from the canteen.

23. At 6am, during the count of the prisoners, the officer in charge and the guard arrived to count us. They promised to send someone to me but they did not do so and did not do anything at all to help me. I remained in the same state until 8.30 am, during which time my fellow prisoners were shouting and calling for the doctor and the prison officer in an effort to get me some medical care. The prison officer agreed, but did nothing.

24. When the Work officer arrived to take the Israeli women prisoners who work in the prison factories, we called her and explained the situation to her. She in turn contacted the prison administration and informed them of what was happening. A second prison officer arrived to take me at 8.30 am, and I was left in the administration hall until they finished the required procedures. I was bleeding heavily during that period and the blood fell on the floor because I did not have a sanitary towel. I started screaming and told them that I was in pain as well as bleeding and that I could not bear it any longer. Therefore, about 10am, they took me back to the hospital.

25. I was treated in the same manner as before. Then they took me to a special section where I found the prison doctor. He examined

me and caused something to come down, and then treated me with a type of solution.

26. After that, they took me to the upper section of the hospital where they brought a nurse to carry out a dilation and curettage operation on me. They brought a piece of paper written in Hebrew which they asked me to sign but I refused. I told the nurse that I was afraid that the miscarriage had been brought about deliberately and I did not want to sign something I was not able to read and understand. Later, I lost consciousness because I was injected with an anaesthetic.

27. I regained consciousness in the afternoon and found myself alone in another room with a male and a female soldier. An hour later, they brought some food which I refused to eat.

28. I was taken back to the prison, where a dispute was going on between the Palestinian women political prisoners and the Israeli criminal prisoners. The Palestinian women were in their rooms and the Israelis were in the prison yard, throwing garbage at the Palestinians and cursing them. The prison officer refused to open the door for me and left me standing in the yard among the Israeli prisoners. I was extremely vulnerable to being attacked. I told her that I had just come from hospital and that I was bleeding and in pain. She took me to the Palestinian prisoners' room.

29. I found out that supper had been served and that there was nothing left for me to eat. I did not eat until breakfast time the next day.

30. The next day, the conflict between the prison officers and the Palestinian prisoners became more serious. The prison administration punished two of the prisoners by putting them in a cell, for trying to strangle one of the guards. The administration imposed a collective punishment, cutting off both the hot and the cold water supplies.

31. I was supposed to take medicine for four days but it was not given to me.

32. Four days after I left hospital, my family came to visit me. They had learned about the miscarriage from the newspapers. They told me that they had contacted the lawyer, Leah Tsemel, who in turn had contacted the prison administration. The administration had informed Leah Tsemel that I had wanted to miscarry. I then realised that the miscarriage had been brought about deliberately, and had not been an accident as I had previously thought.

33. I therefore asked my family to contact the Red Cross and ask them to make a complaint against the prison administration. Three days after that, the Red Cross representative visited me, talked to me and asked me about the miscarriage. She then went to make enquiries of the prison clinic staff, but the clinic was closed (which was most unusual). She promised to bring me a report on the miscarriage and to continue her enquiries a week later.

34. Five days after the visit, my appeal was heard. The court said it would give its decision in one week's time. But after I left the court and was taken back to prison, at about 4.30 in the afternoon, the prison officer informed me that my release had been ordered. I had spent two and a half months in administrative detention.

35. I tried to obtain a copy of the medical report which the Red Cross representative had promised to get, but when I contacted them they refused to give it to me and were unwilling to discuss the subject.

36. After my release from prison, I suffered from pains in my uterus and was given medication by the doctor, who diagnosed me as suffering from inflammation. This went on for two years.

37. I am now pregnant again [July 90] for the first time since the miscarriage. I did not want to get pregnant in the intervening two years.

38. Looking back on my experience in Ramla, I would describe it as emotional (as opposed to physical) torture. I was treated more like an animal than a human being. Nowadays when I see women in hospital who have miscarried, I remember what happened to me in Ramla and it is very painful.

39. Following my release, I experienced a lot of harassment by the army at my home. My husband was arrested and held for one month. I understand that he was told by the security forces to prevent me from working and from going out.

2. Na'ila 'Ayish

Na'ila 'Ayish miscarried during her interrogation, apparently as a result of the physical and psychological abuse to which she was subjected by GSS officers. The case is referred to several times in Chapter Two. See in particular the "Case Study" at the end of Chapter Two, where a statement by Na'ila's lawyer setting out the abuse which led to the miscarriage is quoted in full. The case is only summarized here.

Na'ila, from Gaza, was arrested on 19 February 1987 when she was about five weeks pregnant. (She had a pregnancy test done on 15 February which was positive.) She was 26 and this was her first pregnancy. She was taken to the Russian Compound in Jerusalem on 20 February and her interrogation began the following day. Na'ila says that she told her interrogators from the start that she was pregnant, to which they replied that for them there was no difference between her and a man. She asked repeatedly to be seen by a doctor but was told that this would only be granted if she confessed.

Na'ila was subjected to the types of physical and psychological abuse which are common in interrogations of Palestinian women prisoners. She was placed in *shabah* for long periods of time, with her head covered by a filthy sack. She spent three nights out of doors in *shabah* during the first week, in cold and wet winter weather. One of the interrogators banged her head against the wall on more than one occasion. On another occasion, she was left in a room with the air conditioner on cold. In addition, Na'ila was subjected to sexual threats against her and against members of her family.

Na'ila began to haemorrhage on 22 February, the second day of her interrogation. She informed the interrogators of this, but they told her that they did not believe her. The bleeding continued until the 4th or 5th of March.

A prison doctor did visit Na'ila on 25 February, but he did not examine her. He asked for a urine sample to be taken. According to the lawyer's statement, two samples were in fact taken; but they were not tested on the grounds that they contained blood. The samples, if tested, could have provided the vital evidence as to whether Na'ila's claims to be pregnant were true or not, since the GSS were claiming that she was lying. Na'ila received no further medical attention until 15 March, when she was taken to an Israeli hospital. Here she was given an ultrasound examination which showed that she was not then pregnant.

On 19 March the authorities gave permission for Na'ila to be examined by an independent doctor, Dr. Ahmad Muhtadie. He later gained permission for her to be brought to Augusta Victoria hospital, where he performed a dilation and curettage operation.

He took an endometrial biopsy, part of which was sent to the pathology laboratory at an Israeli hospital (Hadassah, Mount Scopus) while the other part was sent to a Palestinian laboratory. Both laboratories reported that the biopsy showed "early secretory endometrium" corresponding to the seventeenth or eighteenth day of the cycle. From this, together with the case history, Dr Muhtadie concluded that Na'ila 'Ayish had undergone a complete miscarriage between 22 February and 2 March. The bleeding which began on 22 February could not have been a menstrual period, since the biopsy showed that the new menstrual cycle had begun on approximately 2 March.

Na'ila was eventually released on bail and at her trial she was given a suspended sentence as part of a 'plea bargain'.[1]

3. Widad Darwish

Widad Darwish, a journalist from Jerusalem, was arrested on 21 July 1988 in Sultan Suliman street in East Jerusalem, when she was about one month pregnant. It was her third pregnancy. She saw the Border Guards (a police unit with a reputation for brutality) arresting and beating a boy of about 14, for no apparent reason. She went up to ask what was going on. She says that, when she explained that she was a journalist, the Border Guards became angry and began to hit her. She immediately began to shout "I am pregnant, do not beat me!" She says that the Border Guards took no notice, hitting her first on her ears and then all over her body. She says that this continued for quite a long time. Widad was then arrested and taken to the Russian Compound, in the same car as the youth. At the Russian Compound she was taken to the GSS section and interrogated. Her requests to see a doctor were ignored. She was in a lot of pain from the beating and was unable to walk. She was charged with assaulting a Border Guard.

Eventually Widad was allowed to make a statement giving her version of events, in Arabic. She was then taken to the police section of the Russian Compound. Despite her requests to see a doctor, she was locked into a room alone, where she fainted. Eventually she was transferred to the women's cell. There were 28 women in it, sharing 8 beds. Widad had to sit up all night. The women were on hunger strike and Widad received no food and only one cup of water.

The following day Widad was interrogated again, and then released at 1pm.

Widad was taken to hospital immediately by her husband. She could not be X-rayed because of her pregnancy, and was discharged to go home and rest. At 10 o'clock that night, she began to bleed. On the following day the bleeding became heavier. Widad had a pregnancy test done, which gave a positive result. This was her first pregnancy test. She was told by her doctor (Dr Muhtadie) to rest. The bleeding became heavier still and the next day an ultrasound test showed that Widad was no longer pregnant. After doing a dilation and curettage, Dr Muhtadie sent a biopsy to Hadassah Hospital at Mount Scopus, the result of which was "products of conception".

4 'Ayisha al-Kurd of Shabura Refugee Camp, Gaza

'Ayisha was detained in April – May 1988 when she was seven months pregnant with her fifth child. At the time, her husband was already under interrogation regarding involvement in military operations and other matters. 'Ayisha was interrogated about allegedly participating in the former, together with her husband. She agreed to sign a statement in Hebrew on the basis that she would then be released. The statement turned out to be a confession. 'Ayisha was in fact formally released after signing it, but at the prison gate she was re-arrested.

'Ayisha recounts that a strange series of events then took place.

> 10. After I signed the document, I was released. But when I reached the prison gate, I was stopped by some people. They told me to come with them, saying that they wanted to take me somewhere for 10 minutes.
>
> 11. I was then driven to Ashkelon hospital. I was given a scan and I was told that the baby would be a "nationalist freedom fighter", and that he would be born in prison.
>
> 12. I was never released as promised. I was next taken to Ashkelon prison and placed in a tiny cell measuring about 1m x 1.5m. I was held here for the next four days. I was given no food or water,

and was taken out to the toilet only once a day. If I started to fall asleep, guards would come and spit at me and hit me with shoes.

13. During this time, a criminal prisoner took pity on me and used to bring me water, until he was caught. I felt very tired and unwell.

14. I was very worried about my four young children, the oldest of whom was then five years old. They were with my mother-in-law, who is unable to walk.

15. After four days in the small cell, the prison staff took me to Ashkelon hospital. I was seen by doctors. I understood that the doctors wanted to induce the birth of my baby. I saw no reason to do this and so I told them that they must not touch me because it was Ramadan.

16. I was then seen by a doctor who spoke good Arabic. I do not know whether he was an Arab or a Jew. He told me that he was a Gazan and that he was my friend and said that it was time to bring on the birth. I told him I did not want this. He said that if I preferred, he could take me to Nasser hospital in Gaza. I again said "no", I did not want the birth to be induced, since the baby would not be due for another six weeks.

17. During this discussion I heard a female nurse say "she has four children already, she doesn't need another one, let this one die".

18. I was told I was to be taken to a hospital in Tel Aviv. I was made to lie on my stomach in the ambulance, on a stretcher. Neither my hands nor my feet were manacled. I was driven a long distance, taking about an hour. Then the ambulance stopped and I was taken out for a couple of minutes. We were in an empty place, I don't know where it was. I was then put back in the ambulance and driven for another hour. When we stopped we were back at Ashkelon prison.

19. I was put in the small cell again. By this time I had started to bleed. I asked to be taken to the toilet. There I met two Israeli criminal prisoners, and they saw that I was bleeding. They banged on the door to get the attention of the prison officers and shouted out "she's about to give birth". The criminal prisoners told me that probably I would be transferred to Ramla, because Ashkelon prison would want to avoid being held responsible for my giving birth prematurely.

20. I spent that night in the small cell. At 9am the next morning, I was indeed taken to Ramla prison. I was not given the care I needed by the prison officers, but I was placed with the Palestinian women political prisoners and they did their best to look after me.

21. I continued to bleed for three days. Then the bleeding stopped, much to my relief."

'Ayisha al-Kurd's baby was born safely in due course.

Note

1. A plea bargain is an arrangement between the prosecution and the defence whereby the defendant agrees to plead guilty to one or more charges in return for the prosecution offering him or her some concession. The concession may be the dropping of a further charge or, typically in the Israeli military courts, that the prosecution ask the court to pass a lower sentence than they might otherwise have requested it to pass.

Index